The School on the Common

The History of St John's School, Redhill

ALAN MOORE

Front cover: Childen from the 1920s. Back cover: their modern day counterparts.
Above: The original St John's School built in 1845. It stood approximately where the infants' part of the present upper building stands now. Nothing from the pictured building remains.

The School on the Common
First published 2006

Published by Alan Moore

Distributed by St John's School, Redhill, Surrey

Page design by Louisa Swaden

Cover design by Jonathan Spearman-Oxx

Printed by Polestar Wheatons, Exeter

ISBN 0-9546469-2-4

The School on the Common
Contents

Chronology

1843	St John's Church built.
1845	First building of St John's School erected.
1846	Origins of the town of Redhill.
1863	Reigate Borough Council formed.
1884	New lower building erected for Boys' School.
1887	Queen Victoria's Golden Jubilee.
1897	Queen Victoria's Diamond Jubilee.
1901	Death of Queen Victoria. Edward VII came to the throne.
1903	Reigate Council takes over from the Church as the Local Education Authority.
1908	Girls' and infants' departments became a Council School, Boys' department remained Church School.
1910	Original buildings demolished, new upper building erected. Death of Edward VII. George V came to the throne.
1913	50th Jubilee of Reigate Borough Council.
1914-18	World War One.
1935	Death of King George V.
1936	George VI came to the throne.
1939-45	World War Two.
1945	Surrey County Council takes over from Reigate Council as the Local Education Authority.
1952	Queen Elizabeth II came to the throne.
1954	St John's Boys' Church School moved to Sandcross Lane.
1964	Girls' and Boys' Schools merge.
1972	Infants' School merges with Boys' and Girls' School.
1977	Queen Elizabeth II Silver Jubilee.
2002	Queen Elizabeth II Golden Jubilee.
2005	Air raid shelters re-opened.
2006	History of St. John's School published.

The History of St John's School, Redhill 1845 - 2006

Introduction

St John's School is a small, typically English, a seemingly unremarkable school in the south of England. It was founded one hundred and sixty years ago and the period that has since elapsed can be represented as the equal of at least six generations. Thousands of children have passed through the classrooms of hundreds of teachers. Together they lived through some of the most important events in our past.

History is important. St John's may not be *more* important than any other similar school but it is at least *as* important, and if its written history is intact then it can provide a window to the past that others cannot. Fortunately St John's history, although it has gaps, is complete enough to make a detailed look at it fully worthwhile. Reading the records of meetings and events left behind in log-books, minute books and other documents is like travelling back in time, with the difference that no technology need be employed because the technology of the past - pen and ink - have done the work for us. All we have to do is read that which many hands have written. Technology has played its part in the transcription of the data, of course. Where would we be without our photocopiers and computers? When we look back and see how our forebears managed without such things, we wonder how we would cope in their place were we suddenly transported back to join them.

Although the recent turn of the Millennium has turned another page of time there are many parallels between the St John's of old and of today. Many of the problems encountered in the past ring bells with loud familiarity in our minds as we read. But much is different, and it is the differences of attitude and necessity, not simply of time, that make the history so fascinating, the reading so enjoyable, the research so worthwhile. If we could go back we could tell those pupils, teachers and managers of old what has happened since their times, and surely they would be surprised to discover how much we had learnt about them. Who knows how much they could tell us? And tell us some of them do, for once the story reaches the period of living memory so personal reminiscences become available, and many are included to swell the information gained by other means.

The general style of this history is to follow a chronological path, with some subjects dealt with in paragraphs that exhaust a certain amount of their particular subject before returning to the main theme. Also some matters have bearing upon others so it seems better to deal with them together, and appendices contain additional information. The alternative, a purely thematic approach, keeps facts grouped by subject but necessitates frequent returns to years previously dealt with. I hope the method chosen has done the subject justice, while the means adopted to reduce the constant presentation of differing facts has made the narrative easy on the reader.

Alan Moore

Acknowledgements

This book has been produced with the sponsorship of a number of companies and individuals without whose help it would never have seen the light of day. The Staff and Governing Body of St John's are extremely grateful for their generous assistance and are pleased to include their names below.

Heritage Lottery Fund
Watson Wyatt Limited
Redhill Centre for Local and Family History
Stoneman Funeral Services

Special thanks to: -

Marian Cassidy, for her encouragement and support in the writing of this history.
Louisa Swaden for her professional expertise in the production of this book.
The late Maurice Higgins for his early support in the fundraising efforts.
The Air Raid Shelter Committee for their assistance in proof-reading and editing.

Also to the past pupils and friends of the School whose contributions in the form of pictures and reminiscences have greatly enhanced the telling of this story.

All proceeds from the sale of this book will directly benefit St John's School.

The Local Heritage Initiative is a national grant scheme that helps local groups to investigate, explain and care for their local landscape, landmarks, traditions and culture. The Heritage Lottery Fund (HLF) provides the grant but the scheme is a partnership, administered by the Countryside Agency with additional funding from Nationwide Building Society.

Chapter One
The Early Years

The history of St John's School began in the days of Reigate Manor, 23 years before the Borough Council was formed, at a time when the only local church was St Mary's at Reigate and the town of Redhill was not yet in existence.

This was a time when the Church had a hand in civic as well as ecclesiastical affairs via regular organised meetings known as Vestries. On 21st August 1840 one such vestry meeting was held to consider a proposal that £411.12.6 of parish funds be put towards the building of a new church to serve the rising population of a place called Little London, which was how the present St John's area was then known. Other proposals that £100 of the money be put towards improving the access to the new railway station, or filling in holes in the roads and the building of a gallery in St Mary's at Reigate were defeated. More than one site for the church was considered. One was where St John's School now stands but the sub-soil was found to be unsatisfactory for burials and an alternative, on the other side of the road, was chosen.

The Church, built in 1843 and at first called Red Hill District Church after the area of nearby rising common known by that name, was soon consecrated as St John the Evangelist. It was from this time that the name of St John's also came to be used for the area around it and the name of Little London fell into disuse. Within a few years a town was to grow up close to the railway station a mile north of St John's. It was at first called Warwick Town but from 1856 also adopted the name of Red Hill.

That 1840 vestry meeting had additional importance for local children. The London to Brighton Railway had recently been built across part of the common close by and a decision was taken that the London, Brighton & South Coast Railway Company should be made to pay compensation to the churchwardens for the loss of grazing and other rights on that land.

Plans to build a school at St John's were being formulated and an application for financial aid to build the school was submitted to the National Society (in effect the Church of England) on 2nd December 1843 by the incumbent of St John's Church, the Rev. William Pullen, and the Secretary of the School Committee, Thomas Martin of Reigate, for additional funds to make up a shortfall in the total amount required. Funds in hand raised by subscription and church collections at this time totalled £761. This was short of the amount required, which was £1064. The amount anticipated to be

St John's Church as originally built, when it had a fence around it and not the flint wall we see today. This picture dates from 1857, by which time the lane past it had become a much wider road. Washing can be seen on the triangular green formed with the junction of what is today Fountain Road. Picture courtesy Reigate and Banstead Council

forthcoming was £300 but in the event the National Society donated £150, raising the total available for the build to £901. This was still short by £263 of the amount required. There was a further £100 needed for a year's salary for a Master, a Mistress, books etc., but that was to be raised by subscription and the levying a charge of 1d per week per child.

The population of the St John's District, which probably included Meadvale, was given to be 1200. With an eye to expansion the school was to be built to accommodate 100 boys, 100 girls and 100 infants. Existing educational facilities were stated on the form applying for funds from the National Society as being in two small cottages where 40 boys, 20 girls and 60 infants attended. Where they were is not stated but they were probably at Meadvale. Wherever they were they were said to be wholly inadequate. The only other education was Sunday school in St John's Church, where upwards of 60 children attended.

The boys' school room was to be 38 x 17 feet; the girls' schoolroom was to be 26 x 17 feet and the infants 32 x 17 feet. Each was to be 13 feet high. These dimensions are shown on the form to allow six square feet for each pupil but it seems that once the master is standing before the class and room for a stove and cupboards are allowed for then the space per child would be considerably less. Six square feet is defined by the dimensions 2 feet 5 inches by 2 feet 5 inches. Once this is reduced, as stated above, conditions in any one of the classrooms would have been cosy to say the least.

In October 1844, the churchwardens held a local poll to decide what to do with £535.7s compensation granted by the London, Brighton & South Coast Railway Company as a result of their 1840 compensation claim. The decision was to spend one third on the poor rate and two thirds to erect National Schools (the plural referring to the separate Boys', Girls' and Infants' departments) which would seem to more than make up the deficit. However, documents seen at the National Society archives dated 1845 and 1846 also refer to a donation of £200 by the Committee of Council for Education and continued deficits, so the situation is clouded slightly. This may be explained by the fact that although the donations referred to above were promised they were not paid until building works were completed. One letter dated 25th April 1846 asking for financial aid from the National Schools Society refers to the school being in operation for one month yet still in debt. Although it does not clear up the financial situation for us it does put the commencement of teaching children at St John's at March 1846.

The land that the school was built on was part of the waste of the Borough, that is to say common land. As all such land was owned by the lord of the manor it had to be conveyed by deed by Earl Somers and his son, Viscount Eastnor, to the trustees, who were described as the Ministers, Churchwardens and their Successors. In addition the deed, dated 19th June 1845, stipulated that there would be a set of Managers, who would be the Rector of the Parish and the Minister of the District (presumably the Vicar of the main church of St Mary's at Reigate and the Vicar of St John's) plus three individuals named in the deed. This Management Committee was to be renewed when reduced to two or one by death or otherwise. If possible the lord of the manor and the Incumbent of the District (the vicar) were to be Managers at all times.

People involved with the building of the school from the 1843 outset, and whose names appear on some of the earliest documentation, were the Rev. Snelson, Vicar of Reigate, the Rev. William Pullen, the first Vicar of St John's, one William Joshua Tilley, William Price, who was the treasurer and is quite possibly the man after whom Prices Lane is named, and Thomas Martin, who was the Bailiff of Reigate from 1811 to his death in 1867. Their School, now much larger and much altered, today exists as St John's Community School.

St John's School Plans

These plans of St John's School nearly all date from the 1850s so are all of the original building and may be compared with that building in the picture on the inside of the cover. The only ones not dated are one of the ground plans and the section through the gallery. They are in the on deposit at Woking History Centre and due to their delicate nature the staff there would not allow them to be

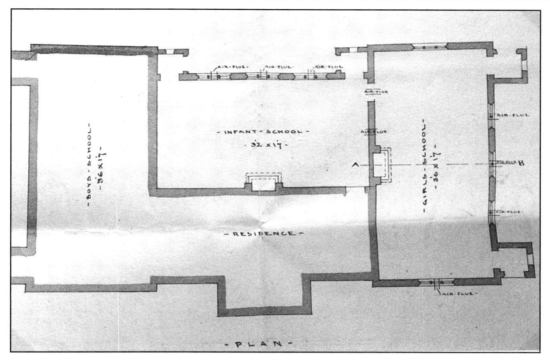

Plan 1. (No date but watermarked 1852). This shows the basic layout of the original School, with the Infants' School situated to the back of the building between the Girls' School on the right and the Boys' School on the left. The Headmaster's residence was in the front of the building. Courtesy Surrey History Centre.

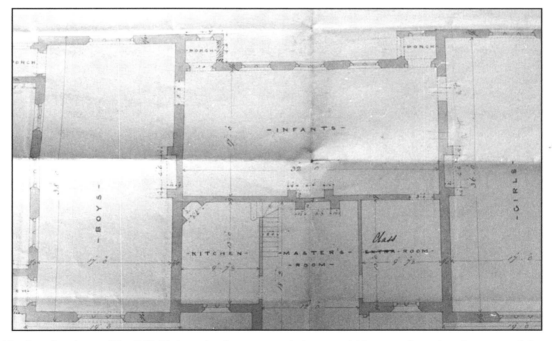

Plan 2. No date but has a 'Redhill, Reigate' reference on it that would have referred to the area of the common and not the town. This is because Redhill was then called Warwick Town and did not begin to assume the name Red Hill or Redhill until after the Post Office moved into Station Road from Whitepost Hill in 1856. This serves to date this plan to the 1850s. This is similar to plan 1 but with more information. The Master's residence had at least three rooms on two storeys in the central front. The central one is marked 'Master's Room', the right hand one 'Classroom', and the left hand one is an upstairs kitchen. What lay under the kitchen is not shown or known. Later a separate house was built with the aid of funds from benefactor Mrs Price (possibly wife of the Mr Price that Prices Lane, Woodhatch, was named after). The central room of the residence then probably became an office. Courtesy Surrey History Centre.

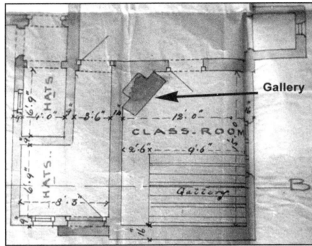

Plan 3 (Dated 1858). This is an extension to the south-west corner of the Boys' School (turn it through 180° and it goes onto the top LH corner of plan 2) consisting of a classroom and two cloakrooms. In the classroom is a gallery, which is shown in more detail in plan 4. The cloakrooms (here marked 'hats' probably because everyone wore a hat in those days) were presumably one for the boys and one for the infants. In the logbook it is recounted how school had to finish early in the winter so that the children could find their clothes, as there was no gas lighting provided in the cloakrooms. As this plan is dated 1858 it would tend to indicate the previous plans are earlier, i.e. before an extension was required. The Gallery was in the classroom indicated.
Courtesy Surrey History Centre.

Plan 4 Gallery construction. Gallery lessons were a part of the curriculum and covered a variety of subjects. Children would sit in the galleries for these lessons where they would have a good view of the teacher and any subject material. A report in this history refers to an Inspector's report that says the children ought to be taught to sit without moving about, but this would seem to have been almost impossible on the hard wood of the galleries unless cushions were placed upon them.
Courtesy Surrey History Centre.

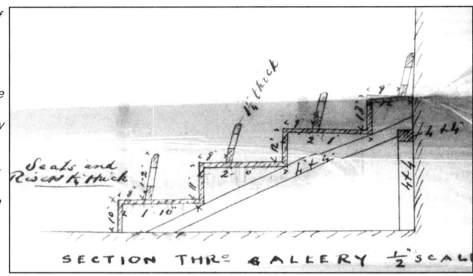

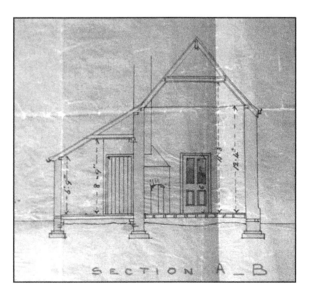

Plan 5. This section through the extension in plan 3 shows the inside of the building. The classroom door is the one leading from it to the main hall, and the cloakroom door also leads into the main hall. The structure to the left of the classroom door is a fireplace that would have warmed the teacher nicely on a cold and frosty morning but the children would have had to wait for the room to heat up overall.
Courtesy Surrey History Centre.

photocopied, only photographed. This was done in the natural light from the large windows of the research area; the shadows formed by the folds in the paper are the reason for most of the tonal variation on the prints.

It ought to be pointed out that the existence of these plans is not proof that the information in them is accurate (in plan 1 the Boys' School and the Girls' School are the same size, whereas in plan 2 the Boys' School is 2' longer). The old school looked very similar to these plans but whether the proposed extension was built is not known. All plans are either dated in the 1850s or have 1850s watermarks, the latter indicating the age of the paper but not the date of the plans.

Enlargement 1861

The first enlargement of the School seems to have been around 1861. Part of that enlargement would presumably have included the original clock tower, as the clock in the present tower is dated 1861 and is reported to be the same clock as originally provided. Additional expansion is said to have occurred in 1881. This is possibly a reference to the building of the Boys' School that actually occurred in 1884.

The Management Committee 1870 - 1876

The earliest known Management Committee minutes date from 1870, a quarter of a century after the formation of the Schools. It is such a shame that knowledge of those first 25 years is so limited. The Committee of Managers running the Schools did so on behalf of the Government, which gave an annual grant based on average attendance, and subscribers, who were people giving additional monies in the form of gifts (56 subscribers are listed in the 1874 report). Probably the law required that there be a Management Committee and that it be representative of the community. No doubt the Church had a considerable say in matters, which was why the Vicar of St John's Church was the Committee Chairman. It is unclear who picked the original Committee, although it could well have been the Parish Vestry. Probably the first Vicar of St. John's was the original chair of the Management Committee. His replacement, the Rev. Henry Gosse, succeeded him as Chairman in 1846, very early in the School's history.

In 1871 the Committee decided to reorganise and make itself more perfectly representative of the subscribers by inviting others to join its number, some of whom accepted. The Committee of Messrs Hesketh, Paine and Whately, with the Rev. Henry Gosse, still the Vicar of St John's, as Chairman, invited Mr W.B.Waterlow (then Mayor) B.Bird Esq., Dr Grabham, W.D.Scott and Mr Reed to join them. The latter declined. Subsequent additions to the Committee are dealt with from time to time in the text.

One of the Managers at a slightly later date was a Captain Marryat, although not the one of literary fame who lived 1792–1848. In May 1878 the rank of our Marryat had advanced to Admiral.

The glaring omission of representation on the Committee was that of the Schools themselves, with none of the staff a member. In order to correct this, and to give the Committee an information source at meetings, it was resolved in November 1871 that either the Master or Mistress be available to answer questions, should there be any. This suggestion seemed to stop short of involving either of those persons in decision making, and not surprisingly the request for a presence was declined. How this was resolved is not clear but the first instance of a question being asked of a staff member was of the Girls' Mistress in Committee in 1876. The minutes record that an answer was received, making it appear that the lady was present.

Local Tradesmen 1870 - 1876

The Committee had responsibility for all aspects of the running of the Schools and used local professional people to carry out work. In October 1870 a tender for a washing closet for girls in a closed porch was requested from Mr Carruthers. When, in March of 1871, the then St John's

The School on the Common

St John's School from the common in 1857. Between School and Church is the Earlswood Asylum. A tall funnelled engine steams on the Brighton line between them.

Boys' Schoolmaster, Mr J.G.Scott, applied for a better class of coal, the Committee Secretary contacted Rickett Smith, coal merchants of Redhill. In March 1871 palings were to be repaired by Mr Comber, who in 1843 had built St John's Church, and in 1872 he was also asked to repair the platform in the clock tower broken by the fall of the clock weight. As a result of this latter incident another Redhill tradesman, Mr Fowle, jeweller and watchmaker, was asked to state his charge for winding and maintaining the clock by the year. His fee of £1.5.0 was accepted.

Local tradesmen would probably have also tendered for extensive repairs proposed in May 1871 to the external fabric of the old School's fences, gates and WC plus the new School and its dwelling house. The cost was £178.3.9, although circulars sent out to the subscribers realised only £57 and it was necessary to send out a second circular advising of the poor result. The money was still not fully raised and it can only be assumed that limited work was done, for the minutes do not mention the subject again until 1876, when work was carried out to the walls.

Another job no doubt carried out by a local tradesman was the emptying of the cesspit. Manager Mr Oram had the responsibility of arranging this when in 1875 the Committee asked him to find out if the overflow from the cesspit could be connected to the sink drain. That such an action should even have been considered seems appalling today but this was an age when main drainage for both surface water and sewage was something new. The land for the sewerage works at Earlswood was not bought until 1867 and the sewerage scheme for the Borough as a whole not finished until 1876. Many people thought at the time that the laying of such pipes was excessively expensive and that the system of cesspools was perfectly adequate. Fortunately the School Management was not so persuaded and the Schools were connected to the new main sewer in 1876. We shall see later in this history that disease in the form of many illnesses almost eradicated today was a major source of absenteeism, even death. Moreover it affected all social classes almost equally. The reason in many cases was the lack of hygiene, especially the cleanliness of drinking water that was not sufficiently separated from sewage outlets and overflows.

The Budget and School Boards 1871

The 1871 budget only just balanced. 1872's budget was to be £40 deficient and the situation was to get worse before it got better. This caused the Management Committee to bring the matter to the attention of Surrey Church Association, pointing out the danger of the school lapsing into the hands of a School Board. Education locally had so far been mainly administered and provided by a number of charitable, voluntary, religious and private organisations. Following the 1870 Education Act Government Inspectors had, from time to time, pronounced unfavourably upon some of these groups and the possibility of a School Board replacing them reared its head at these times. This would mean that unless the schools concerned improved a local School Board would be elected with powers to draw on the rates, improve or rebuild schools and enforce attendance by children aged between 5 and 13. This was opposed partly because the rates would go up and partly because religious groups taught their own brand of religious education and feared a too general approach to the subject might be introduced. Schools therefore carried out improvements as necessary, raising the money as best they could, as the Surrey Church Association gave money for new schools but not for repairs to existing ones.

The subject of the School Board was soon back on the agenda, this time put there by Mr Hesketh in December 1871. He put forward a resolution for future discussion. *'The Managers of the National School of St John's, Redhill, are of the opinion that it is expedient that a School Board be formed for the Borough of Reigate and that they form their opinion mostly on the necessity which exists in many cases for the compulsory powers under the Elementary Education Act to be exercised.'*

Mr Hesketh perhaps felt that the Council would make a better job of running the Schools than the present Management Committee. After due discussion he must have found himself in a considerable minority on the subject and withdrew the resolution. That other School Management Committees felt the same as the majority at St John's is evidenced by the following from the *Reigate Journal* of 27th February 1872:

Opening of New St Matthew's Boys' School by Bishop of Winchester

The general desire to further the cause of education, and a specific desire to avoid the establishment of a school board, with its possible tending to secular education, have led to the erection of a new National School for Boys for the district of St Matthew's, Redhill, just as the same causes led but recently to the establishment of a new Wesleyan day school in the same district. The new building has been erected by Mr Curruthers under contract from designs gratuitously furnished by Mr Hesketh of the Mount, Redhill.

Mr Hesketh was clearly well involved in school development in Redhill.

Use of the Premises by Others 1870 - 1884

In September 1871 a lock was fitted to the Mistress's back door to prevent the school water supply being used by others during the holidays. It is not known what the supply referred to was but as the school did not at this time have the benefit of piped water there must have been a well. Crockerty Well was on the triangle of grass between the southern wall of the Church and Pendleton (then Union) and Fountain Roads, but it seems likely that an additional well, perhaps more than one (the Workhouse had three) would have existed on the school premises.

Evening School and Other Matters 1870s and 1880s

In November 1871 discussions on sharing gas costs with a Working Men's Club that used the Boys' premises resulted in an additional gas lamp being provided. The St John's Evening Entertainment Society used the premises fortnightly for lectures, concerts and readings certainly from 1879. At the same time choir practice was held in the school out of hours under the supervision of one Mr Pringuer, and a string band used it weekly. In all cases the charges were always said to be to cover costs of heating, lighting, wear and tear and cleaning, with no mention of any profit to be made by the School. This changed when the new Boys' School was built in 1884 when £2.2.0 was the rate for use of its main hall.

A part of the school that could also come under Government supervision was the Evening School, at which teaching was done in early years mainly by Miss Hesketh and Miss Gosse. The Committee decided in 1871 that it should be independent and be run for the benefit of the Parish. This changed when the Janneys came to be the Head Teachers, as they were allowed to run the evening school as a private venture and keep the proceeds for themselves. This continued under the Jinks' Headship, a condition of their employment being that private tuition only be carried out evenings and Saturdays. More about the Janneys and the Jinks later.

The School on the Common

As expected the prime source of pupils for the Boys' School and Girls' School was St John's own Infants' School but pupils also came from elsewhere. In December 1887 Mabel Taylor, a private school pupil, was admitted and in January of 1889 twenty-seven girls were admitted from Meadvale plus three others, making a total roll of 210. This put the attendance figures up to a new high of 174 and an additional coat-peg stand had to be ordered. (The difference between the number on roll and actual attendance figure being due to non-attendance of children due to illness, bad weather and other reasons). The following October plans for extra desks were being considered. In November 1901 Agnes T.McKay, whose parents being Roman Catholic did not want her instructed in Catechism and the Prayer Book of the Church of England, was admitted.

Children under five were generally admitted but during the winter of 1902 a few very young children were not being sent until the bad weather was over. Now and then a child would be well over that age and not have been to school before, as in the case of Maude Rice in 1894 when she was admitted at eight years of age to her first school. The logs of 31st August 1903 also record, *'Admitted girl of eight who knows nothing',* and another entry reads, *'Admitted a boy aged six and a half who does not know a letter.'* In the early years this was a common occurrence.

One group of children not admitted to St John's for many years was those from the Workhouse. At the end of 1871 Mr Clutton, presumably a member of the Guardians, a group administering the Workhouse, wrote to ask that its children be admitted. The Committee declined on the grounds that they had neither the accommodation nor the funds to allow this. In the 1880s Mr Carter Morrison, the then Chairman of the Guardians, asked again that the 40 children then at the Workhouse should be admitted. The Managers offered to take the girls and the infants but refused the boys because the new Boys' School was licensed for 250 boys and this was the number on roll, so there was no room. Because of this the request was withdrawn but renewed the following year for 25 children. St John's situation was now worse because not only was the Boys' School full but the Girls' School had taken all the older girls from the Meadvale School (see reason for this under heading 'Meadvale School') and had 217 on the register. A suggestion was made to the Board of Guardians that the children from the Workhouse be sent to St Matthew's School where there seemed to be ample room. A check of St Matthew's logs or the Board of Guardians' minutes might reveal if this was done, otherwise it would seem that the Workhouse children received little or no education.

The intention of the Guardians must have been to make yearly applications, a strategy that eventually worked, for in February 1889 the Rev. J.M.Gordon called at the school to discuss admittance of Workhouse children. A number of infants, 10 girls and three or four boys were admitted for the first time on 13th May 1889. Admissions continued for Workhouse children but by the end of WW1 an Orphanage had been established for boys and girls at Hardwick Road, Meadvale and children were no longer cared for at the Workhouse. Children from here continued to attend St John's and were often referred to as 'Home Boys' or 'Home Girls' by other children.

In 1873 the average attendance was 78 boys, 79 girls and 64 infants, a total of 221 children, with more than this number actually on roll. In 1877 the figures were: -

	Boys	Girls	Infants	Total
On Roll	129	107	112	348
Av. Att.	99	71	71	241

In 1886 the girls' official accommodation was 256 but attendance varied from 100 to 130. By 1888 the attendance in Girls' School was at its highest ever at 162. It continued to rise through the years until 1894 when two classrooms in the Girls' School had to be enlarged after an Inspector's report said they were too small. In 1895 attendance was at 216 with the Workhouse girls absent and 276 on roll.

Home For Dinner

For almost all of the first hundred years in the life of the school children went home for their dinner every day. According to information given at a talk to the Holmesdale Club by Miss Dorothy Lee, a lady whose family had lived in Redhill since 1878, one way that children living near to the upper part of the Brighton Road knew when it was time to return was when they heard the toot of the Brighton coach arriving at the Somers Arms Inn at the bottom of Mill Street. This story, if accurate, would mean that the Brighton coach still ran regularly in the 1880s, forty years after the coming of the railway that had generally replaced coaching, and before the Somers Arms moved to Reffells Bridge and the Rev. Gosse took over the building as St John's vicarage. If inaccurate it could have been some other signal that was heard, such as a hooter at the gas works that used to sound several times a day at set times, or a similar one at the Redhill Laundry next to the school.

Due to the lunch break, attendance began to be marked twice a day, morning and afternoon, creating two daily attendances where there had previously only been one. In the days when rewards for good attendance were given, total yearly attendances of four hundred and above were achieved by some children in a single year.

Supplies 1870s and 90s

When teaching aids and supplies were required for the school the Master or Mistress, which was how the Headteacher was then called, had to provide a list of their requirements for the Management Committee. The kinds of things requested were foolscap and blotting paper by the ream, pencils by the dozen boxes, slate pencils and chalk by the box, dictation books (ruled, with marbled covers), subject books and bibles, also by the dozen. Slates (large 10" x 8", small 8½" x 6", framed and unframed) also came in twelves, ink by the gallon, and penholders and nibs by the gross. Charts and maps came singly. Blackboards and cupboards were ordered from time to time plus various other items such as registers and other stationery.

In the 1870s most general items seem to have been provided in spite of budget difficulties but some larger items, such as cupboards and desks, had decisions deferred. A pattern of desk ordered for the Boys' School in 1875 was the 'Osborne Reversible' in 6' lengths, each accommodating four children (18" each). Manager Mr Hesketh agreed to take on the task of securing the new desks at a discount (£33.2.0) while Mr Oram's task was to get the best possible price for the old ones (he got £1). The money for the purchase was obtained from additional donations as the school budget was running at a deficit of £60 at the time.

The Infants' School in the 1890s and into the next century received supplies annually. In 1901 this comprised reading books, pictures (one set of silkworm, rattlesnake and pig, for example), crayons, slates, slate pencils, slate pencil sharpeners, counters, 5 packets of embroidery cards, 4 doz. word building cubes, 3 doz. B.B.sponges, 10 packets of letters, exercise books and pencils, 1 doz. ordinary sewing needles, 3 packets of Roman sewing needles, sewing cotton, 1 bundle of

Crewel wool, 6lbs rainbow cotton, 2lbs. white cotton, scissors, penknife, 4 yards of Burke's calico, 1 gross thimbles, 6 packets 4" paper, 12 yards of ravellings and 1 ball of Macramé twine. Other items received included inkstands, ball frames, 7 packets of dotted patterns, 1 gross of red bone beads, 1 bundle of coloured beads, 1 china dinner set, 6 packets of paper for paper folding, a quire of cutting out paper, blackboard cleaner and tin of composition, 1 bundle of Shetland wool, 1 set of knives and forks, 1 set of Newmann's films, 6 doz. knitting needles, Excelsior knitting cotton, coloured chalk, 12 sets of flat braids, 6 tumblers, music leaflets, T squares and a modulator. The list was formidable. A note in the Girls' School logs of September 1902 records additionally, *'A heliograph has been purchased and is in use.'* The presence and purpose of some items is self-explanatory but the writer is unable to explain what others were or to what use they were put.

Curriculum, Examinations and Achievement 1874 - 1902

Singing was one subject taught in the early days and examined by Her Majesty's Inspector. From 1874 drawing lessons began to be given in place of singing, although in 1890 HM Inspector's assistant again examined the school in singing.

In its role as a Church of England School religious education probably took a front seat in time allocated to its teaching and was the subject of yearly inspections by the Diocesan Inspector. The Vicar of St John's Church visited the school regularly to give scripture lessons to the older children. The diocesan examinations were held each July with children being tested in the Old and New Testaments, comprehension of the Church Catechism, the Prayer Book, repetition and written work. Some parts of the Diocesan Inspector's reports show interesting attitudes towards discipline and religious instruction, for example:

1896/7 *'Children need to be taught to sit and stand without moving their arms, heads and bodies about and shuffling their feet'*

1897/8 *'Children suffer from the teacher's over-anxiety. The children are talked to too much. Good work is done by the babies but some lessons on practical duties and abstract virtues (as per syllabus) might be introduced into the Old and New Testament narrative.'*

1898/9 *'The little ones have received a great deal of instruction and are interested in the lessons. It is difficult to gauge their knowledge as they take their cue from one or two especially intelligent members of the class. They know an unusually large amount of repetition which they are inclined not to say but to sing.'*

1901 *'Miss Spurway has maintained a motherly, earnest and thoroughly religious teaching till the last. She has done very valuable service here.'* ('till the last' referred to Miss Spurway, Mistress for 24 years, leaving the school that December)

Children were sometimes put down a Standard (which was how a class, or a year was referred to) if they were not doing very well. Other subjects included the three Rs, geography, and for the girls needlework, knitting and classes in cutting out petticoats. In 1888 the Rev. Gooch was contemplating starting a girls' cookery class. Science and art were not omitted for they were mentioned at the 1889 prize giving. School exams were held monthly and were administered by the teaching staff.

Academic standards were difficult to assess but with the amount of disruption to the school year through a multitude of causes they were probably understandably low at times. When Julia Allen, a Pupil Teacher, was off sick in 1889 Mrs Jinks took Standard III and found a considerable number of children below standard, noting: *'Some were very backward when admitted; some are naturally dull; some have had considerable sickness'.* It may be that Mrs Jinks continued to keep an eye on that class because a week later she was recording that discipline was also poor due to *'the apparent inability of their teacher to keep order'.* (Pupil Teachers were apprentice teachers usually not long out of school themselves.)

In1890 evening classes in French and elementary science were attended by 40 girls in at 1/-each and in November 1899 ten girls were examined in the Boys' School for 'labour certificates'.

Visitors

As well as the Attendance Officer, the Vicar, the Chairman of the School Managers, the Diocesan Inspector and Her Majesty's Inspector of Schools, there were visitors who were like Friends of the School and are referred to on one occasion only as 'Superintendents', on another as 'Subscribers to Needlework' but generally as 'Lady Visitors'. These were local people who took an interest in various aspects of the curriculum. Ladies visited the Girls' School to give instruction in knitting and embroidery. They judged the girls' output once a year and awarded prizes for the best work. Sometimes one would visit and the girls would sing songs for them.

Discipline 1871 - 1881

It might be thought that adults at this time generally ruled children with the proverbial rod of iron and none dare step out of line. This was obviously not universally so, however, for damage to the school clock prompted the strong message from the 1871 management Committee that any St John's boy found stone throwing was to be flogged or, if not from the School, handed over to the police. The clock must have been an attractive target for in January of 1877 the Committee was still discussing steps to be taken to prevent stones being hurled at it.

Punishment in 1871 for two boys, Parfitt and Knight, for 'robbing' from the school premises was determined by the Committee to be carried out by their fathers flogging their sons with a birch rod in front of some of the Managers and some other boys. The fathers' consent to this was sought and not surprisingly declined as the boys had already been flogged once. The Committee decided that the fathers were to be told that the boys could return to school but the Master would make a public statement about them and the boys would stand by themselves until the end of school when they would be told they were forgiven. (Somehow it seems a little late to forgive *after* a flogging and public humiliation!)

Two girls named Turner were also in trouble at the same time, their mother being told that unless she agreed to such punishment as the Committee thought fit they would not be re-admitted to school. Vandalism from boys not attending St John's was also reported, with school windows broken and paths 'wired' (presumably to trip passers-by).

Two matters before the Committee in early 1875 concerned whether the Master should under any circumstances use the cane in the Girls' School and whether caning on the head was permissible. Why these items appeared on the Managers' agenda is not stated but the fact that they came up at all suggests that they were possible courses of disciplinary action. In the event the Managers unanimously decided both in the negative, and most of them expressed their dislike of any use of the cane in the Girls' School. The following November there was a complaint of caning on the head in the Boys' School; the Master's excuse being that the blows fell on the pupil's head by accident. He was told by the Managers to be more careful in future. Then, in the following month, the subject of caning in the Girls' School arose again. It was resolved unanimously by the Managers, *'That caning in the Girls' School be strictly prohibited.'* (underlining as in original text). The Master and Mistress involved were Mr and Mrs Janney, who seem to have been keen on corporal punishment and had to be reined in by the Managers.

Pupil Teachers

Pupil teachers carried out five years training at a school before going to a college for a further two years. They entered into a signed agreement that could be terminated by either side under laid down conditions. Henry Turner was a Pupil Teacher at St John's at the same time as Emily Buckland, also a Pupil Teacher, and the two married. It is through Emily's family that the following paper has survived.

The School on the Common

A religious knowledge examination certificate attained by Henry Turner during his period as a Pupil Teacher. The background colour of original certificate is a very strong blue with impressive decoration.

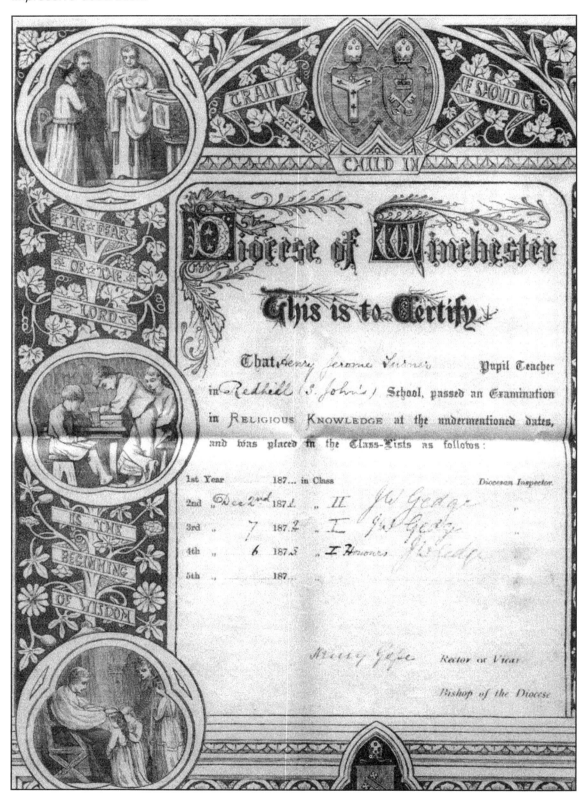

Grateful thanks to Clare Terry for permission to reproduce this.

Chapter Two
Change and Growth

Staff 1843 - 1875

There are few records for staff before 1870. In a booklet on the history of St John's Church, Mr Rose, a former choirboy, says that prior to 1850 the Schoolmaster of St John's, Mr Dinner, led the boys and girls in singing. The census of 1861 tells us that at that time the Master was Edwin Good, aged 28, and the Mistress was his wife, Elizabeth, of the same age. Apart from the fact that they were both born in Wiltshire, nothing more is known of them. In October 1870 school records tell us that Mr Hale resigned as Master of the Boys' School, and Mr John Scott of Battersea Training College was appointed in his place at £60 per annum. Mr Scott, mentioned in chapter 1, appears in the 1871 census. He was aged 20 and had been born in Stoke. The census also shows us that Martha Vic and Fanny Loveless, both aged 23, were Mistresses. The latter came from Lambeth, and also from Lambeth, and also shown living at the school but without occupations, are 80-year old Mary Terry and her daughter Elizabeth, who was unmarried and aged 50. A second daughter aged 62 is shown as a dressmaker. In the early 1900s, Mr Rose, a Redhill tradesman, was quoted in a Surrey Mirror article as saying that he remembered every headmaster of the school; unfortunately for us no names were given.

In April 1872 Miss Vic resigned as Mistress of the Girls' School and Miss Tilley became the new Mistress. Around this time Infants' Mistress Ellen Tracy of Whitelands College was appointed. Both Mistresses received £40 pa and the Master £60 pa. Salaries were paid quarterly with the School's financial year starting on May 1st. (The author considered including a list of all teachers whose names were noted during research. The reason that it was not included was that a 155 year list would run to enough pages to warrant a chapter of its own! An appendix of Heads appears at the end of the book)

The School premises grew to include accommodation for the Boys' School Master and Girls' School Mistress in the form of two houses. A look at the size of the present school buildings gives an idea of the relative smallness of the learning accommodation when two houses were also present. In 1872 the Committee considered the decorative order of the Mistress's house and ordered her sitting room to be papered. At the same meeting the Master's sitting room was to be supplied with a carpet. The houses were not the same size and in October 1873 the Master asked to occupy the larger house as he had just got married. This was acceded to but the Committee reserved the right to make new arrangements about the houses should the Girls' Mistress, Miss Tilley, resign her post (note this point). They also stated that from then on furniture provision and repair would not be their responsibility and reserved for their own use for meetings, *'the large room at present occupied by the Infants' Mistress, the Master to have use of it at other times and to keep it in good order'* (Committee minutes 8th April 1873). The word 'occupied' might have meant that she used it as a daytime office, or she could have lived in it, as part of the conditions of employment included accommodation for her (although her accommodation was referred to as 'rooms' in Committee minutes of 20th October 1873).

Miss Tracy resigned her Infants' Mistress post to go to Mickleham School and as from 1st September 1873 a temporary Infants' Mistress, Miss Frew, took up the post until filled permanently by Miss Kate Denner. At this time the average attendance was 78 boys, 79 girls and 64 infants, a total of 221 children, with something a little more than this actually on roll.

In February 1874 the news of the impending resignation of Mr and Mrs Scott was received. But who was Mrs Scott? The Committee minutes had previously not mentioned such a person although if she too was minuted as resigning then she must have been in the School employ. Also, it was recorded that the resignation was not acceptable unless the Committee was then suited with a new Schoolmaster _and Mistress_ (Committee minutes 7th February 1874), so Mr Scott must have married Miss Tilley (explaining also the point noted earlier).

Even more revealing information is found in the Committee's reply to a Government questionnaire about teachers' conduct, character and attention to duty. They wrote, _'We have no fault to allege against Mr and Mrs Scott which we discovered during their attendance at the school but we have since they left discovered that a child was born by Mrs Scott on the 28th December 1873, they having been married on the 30th September 1873, showing that impropriety had taken place before marriage.'_

Giving birth in the school holidays was surely not sufficient to conceal the preceding pregnancy, so how could the School Managers have been unaware of the situation? The answer to this is in the 1874 report, which states, _'The_ (Girls') _School suffered much from the late Teacher's illness'._ It might seem, then, that the wool was pulled over Managers' eyes, but surely in that day and age they would have had to have been very remote from the School not to hear something of the truth of the matter. This might well have been the case for it was in July of 1875 when the Committee passed a resolution that one of their number be appointed a visitor each month. Was the timing of this a coincidence or was it as a result of the Managers realising that they were not as aware of how the School was conducting itself as they should be? Unfortunately for us the comments of each visiting Manager were not entered in the Committee minutes but kept in a separate book, the whereabouts of which is unknown. (With reference to the name of Scott: on the Annual Report of 31st May 1874 the name of Committee member Mr W.D.Scott has a line through it as though he had resigned from the Committee very close to that time, i.e. after it had gone to print. The timing corresponds very closely with the resignation of Mr Scott the Boys' schoolmaster, raising the question were they one and the same person? W.D.Scott became a management committee member a year after Mr Scott became Master, but when the Master was employed he was entered as Mr J.G.Scott in the minutes, not W.D. Either there is a mistake in the minutes or there was more than one Mr Scott).

The search for a new master culminated in another married couple, Mr and Mrs Janney, being employed and commencing their duties on 13th April 1874. There was soon a complaint against Mr Janney's interference in the affairs of the Infants' School in a letter of resignation by Miss Denner. She left during Christmas 1875 but not before the Committee found that although she had overstated her case Mr Janney had indeed exceeded his office in his treatment of her. What precisely this meant is not clear but at the same meeting at which this conclusion was arrived at the Committee agreed it should meet monthly (to keep a tighter grip on things?). They also resolved that water should be laid on to the Infant Mistress's house, and that the school materials for

A view of St John's from the West. What is now Pendleton Road is still an unmade lane. A covered wagon, similar to that seen on the picture of the original 1845 building, stands on the right. The top of the St John's clock tower can be seen above the houses on the left. The picture dates from around the turn of the century.

the Boys' and Girls' Schools should be kept separate. This last item might have been what the trouble had been about but if the proposed improvement to the water supply served to annoy the departing Mistress it probably did so not as much as the knowledge, if she became privy to it, that her replacement, Miss Scott (yet another by this name) had negotiated £60 pa for herself and so would be doing the same job as her predecessor for a reward of half as much again.

Regarding the Management Committee proposal about monthly meetings, this did not seem to happen, for in 1880 there were only four management meetings in the year, in 1890 there were none at all and in 1891 there was only one. Between 31st December 1894 and 1st October 1896, a span of 21 months, there were no meetings at all, and Major Foster's proposal that the Management Committee meet once a quarter was only carried by the casting vote of the Chairman. Perhaps the Management Committee members met under other circumstances, ie casually or at sub-committees, and found this sufficient.

The 1875 proposal concerning water also fell on stony ground as the Caterham Spring Water Company was not prepared to lay pipes to the School, so the improvement was not carried out at this time. It transpired early in 1876 that it was the Master's job to arrange for the infants' WC to be cleaned, so separation of the schools was not properly achieved. In another sense separation *was* achieved as a month later the privy in the girls' playground was divided into two with an additional door provided, presumably separating them for boys and girls. The subject of water being connected to the Mistress' house was again raised with the additional provision of water for the children to drink. Apparently, up to this time there had been none available to them.

Mr and Mrs Janney resigned their relative positions in July 1876 after two years three months at the School. Their places went to Mr Jinks of Bishop's Hull School in Taunton and Miss Turner of Hungerford National School. Miss Turner was about to marry Mr Jinks, so once again a married couple would be Master and Mistress. Anticipating the probable course that nature might take in this circumstance (and remembering the 'illness' of Mrs Scott) a condition imposed upon the couple by the Committee was that should the new Mistress be incapacitated from attending in School a substitute should be supplied by her without expense to the Committee. This and another condition that Pupil Teacher F.Smith was to live in their house were accepted and the Jinks took up their relative positions at Michaelmas 1876. This was the beginning of a settled period, Mrs Jinks remaining for 25 years, retiring in 1901, Mr Jinks continuing as head of the Boys' School until 1919, a period of over 42 years.

More about the Budget - Attendance and Fees

Money came to the School from three principle sources: a Government Grant, donations and fees paid by the parents of the pupils. The grant depended upon two things, the first being attendance levels. Absenteeism was a problem not just because the children's education was interrupted but because the School grant was paid on average attendance, something which explains the early role of the Attendance Officer and the stringent application of the sending out of irregular attendance forms to parents.

The Annual Grant was made up as per this example of the grant of 1886 for the Girls' School:

	£-s-d	
Fixed Grant	4-6	Paid on Average Attendance of **120**
Merit	3-0	
Needlework	1-0	
Singing	1-0	
On percentage of passes	7-10	
Class subjects - English	2-0	
Geography	2-0	
Sub-total	1-1-4	Total grant including £2 for Pupil Teacher. - **£130**

The School on the Common

The Management Committee considered the matter of absenteeism each 1st of May. (From 1873 the financial year began 1st May; from 1886 the financial year ran from November 1st to October 31st.) On this date in 1874 it could see no remedy, but two years later an attendance incentive was found. It was decided that £5 would be divided among those children achieving 400 or more attendances during the year and that all those achieving 250 or more attendances be given a treat in the form of a trip out to Box Hill or other location. In fact it took the form of an excursion to Brighton in 1878, to Crystal Palace in 1880, and in 1881 a steamer trip on the Thames. It was a scheme that with some modification would continue until the treats were cancelled in 1883. The reason given for the cancellation was that it was universally a system restricted to Sunday Schools, but the school budget was overdrawn at the time and money needed to be raised for enlarging the premises. As the Subscribers were asked for money for both treats and enlargement, the probability was that the former was sacrificed in order to make the them look more favourably upon the latter.

An Act of 1876 that must have given powers to local authorities to ensure children went to school had the January 1877 Management Committee resolving, *'That the Chairman be requested to represent to the Town Council the earnest desire of the Managers of St John's Schools that the provisions of the new Act should be put in force so as to secure the attendance of boys and girls at the elementary schools of the Borough'.* It may have been this same Act that provided three years free education for children gaining an examination certificate of honour; something achieved by pupil Albert Room in 1877.

Around this time, 1874-5, occurred the death of Mrs Price, who had defrayed the cost of building the Boys' School and the Master's House. (It is believed that she may have been the lady whose husband's name lives on in Prices Lane, Woodhatch.)

As already noted, fees were payable by the parents of the children in attendance. Up to 1st February 1875 the weekly rate was 2d for one child, 4d for two children, 6d for three children, 7d for four children and 8d for five, with an additional 1d per child in the top two classes of the Boys' and Girls' Schools. After this date the fee was altered to be a flat 2d per child until raised again in 1878 to 3d for Girls and Boys and 2d for infants. A fourth child was free as long as its siblings attended regularly, and if they did not their absence became the subject of investigation by the then Attendance Officer, Mr Apted, of Reigate. When the new Boys' School was erected in 1884 the system was again altered to 3d for labourers' children and 4d, 6d or 9d for employers and owners of property depending on the means of the parents. All infants were 2d. In Standard VI no child was to pay less than 6d. In 1885 fees were increased to 4d or 6d to children of tradesmen and children over Standard V according to means. All amounts were payable weekly in advance.

In 1870 the Management Committee had turned down an application for fee reduction by a scholar from the Girls' School. On 11th January 1887 the Rev. J.M.Gordon arranged for the reduction of the fees for some poor children in Standard VI. The following March it was recorded that absences were in part due to the inability of some families to pay the fees, which was, of course, a self-defeating part of the system. Fees were eventually abolished, although a Girls' School log entry of 18th July 1888 states; *'School fees given up today',* this must have been an error, or have a different meaning to the obvious one, for it was not until August 1891, three years later, that the Management Committee actually discussed the matter, referring to a new Education Act that came into force on September 1st of that year. This is borne out by an entry in the 1891 Infants' log stating that the Rev. J.O.Gooch visited to say that children were to be admitted free as from that date. This was made possible by the fact that the Government was offering 10/- per child against the 13/2d it actually cost per year to educate a child at St John's. The Management's remedy to make up the shortfall was to no longer charge fees but to accept the Government's offer and charge for books and stationery. On 4th September 1891 circulars were sent to parents about the cessation of school fees in the future but adding that a charge of 3d or 6d a month would be made for books and stationery.

Only four sets of parents officially requested the lower amount because of their reduced circumstances but there was general dissatisfaction all round with the new charges. As a result, and within two weeks, the sum was modified to 1d per week per child for everyone. The original notices put out by the school, plus the subsequent amendment, follow. Ironically an entry in the Girls' School log only sixteen months later (27th January 1893) notes that girls were more irregular than when they paid fees.

The other thing the grant depended upon was the result of Her Majesty's Inspector's annual examination. If any subject result was deemed to be of sufficiently low standard the grant for that subject could be withheld until the situation improved. Similarly, if a Master or Mistress was not of sufficient standard then a part of the grant could also be withheld.

S. John's National Schools

The Management of S. John's National Schools have resolved to accept the provision offered by the new Education Act, and to make their Schools free. The school pence will therefore now be discontinued, but, with the approval of the Education Department, a charge of 3*d.* or 6*d.* a month, for books and stationery, will be made to children in the Boys' and Girls' Schools. This payment will be collected on the first Monday in each month. The first payment will be Due on Monday next, September 7th.

S. John's Schools, Redhill
September 4th, 1891

S. John's National Schools

As some dissatisfaction has been expressed with the existing arrangement, Which was adopted in the hope of lightening the burden of the worst-paid classes of the community, the Managers have resolved to follow the example of other National Schools in the neighbourhood, and to charge in future 1*d.* a week for every child attending this Boys' or Girls' School. This charge will come into operation on Monday, October 5th when the first weekly pence will be collected.

October 1st, 1891

The notices about revised charges as sent out by the School in 1891. The capital S. instead of St normally used in the St John's title is how the notices were printed. Based on originals at Surrey History Centre.

Enlargement of the Schools, Staff, Budgets and School Boards 1878 - 1882

Correspondence from Reigate solicitor Mr Carter Morrison and the Government's Education Department was received in May 1878, putting pressure on the Management Committee to accept a School Board at a time when the budget was £125 in deficit. In order to avoid such an imposition the Committee wrote to the Railway Company (as Redhill was an important railway junction there were quite a few children of Railway employees) and richer incumbents in the area asking for subscriptions to make up the School's income by £50 pa. The railway declined to subscribe and at the same time Mr and Mrs Jinks asked for, and were granted, increases of £10 and £5 respectively (and they got another £5 each in September 1879). In an apparent cost-cutting exercise Mr Burton, the new and first-ever Assistant Master, was told his services were not required after Christmas. A replacement Assistant Master, Mr Burbidge late of St Mark's School, was employed at £1 per week when it became difficult to find Pupil Teachers in 1880.

In April 1879 Mr Hesketh put forward a proposition to enlarge the Schools but the Committee was not disposed to entertain it. Clearly Mr Hesketh thought there was a need for expansion and perhaps the rest of the Committee thought so too, but with the budget still in arrears they probably felt that finance (or lack of it) was too great a restriction.

In July 1882 it was proposed to get the opinion of a surveyor on the bad state of the Master's house and school buildings. Mr Hesketh's offer to make an assessment himself in his capacity as an architect as well as a Manager was accepted by the rest of the Committee. At the same meeting Mr Bourne proposed that an estimate be prepared for the cost of enlargement of the Schools and a special appeal be made to the residents of the neighbourhood. The Rev. Gosse made a counter proposal that instead of enlargement a new Infants' School should be built at Earlswood. These discussions show the matter was becoming even more pressing than since Mr Hesketh's withdrawn proposal three years before. At the next meeting the estimate asked for revealed that the cost of enlargement would be about £2,000. Discussion was postponed because of a meeting at Reigate the very next day, suggesting that the subject of a School Board was once again in the air (if it had ever gone away).

At the February 1882 School prize-giving that took place in the boys' schoolroom, with 100 adults plus children from the upper standards present, bibles were presented for good behaviour to children who were leaving, and money was given to those with for good attendance records. The Rev. Gosse said that the although the schools needed expanding and the financial situation was not good these were problems for the Managers, not the parents, who ought to be pleased that their children had such a good school to go to.

The School Managers were quoted in the local paper the following week as saying that £2000-2500 was needed for repairs and enlargement but only £951 had so far been raised. It seems that either the suggestion of Mr Bourne that an appeal be made had been implemented or fund raising had been going on for some time and had not been mentioned in Management Committee minutes (which is not surprising, as meetings were as irregular as ever).

The Clock Tower

The Rev. Gosse however, still did not seem to be fully convinced about enlargement, saying at the December committee meeting that the Master's house should be repaired and the existing school buildings put in temporary repair instead of expending a large sum. In March 1882 Mr Hesketh said that temporary repairs to the house would be of no permanent benefit. He also said the clock tower was very dangerous. A decision was taken to get a builder to tender for buttresses to support the clock tower and to support the structure while they were built. The Infants' Mistress offered to move into lodgings and let the Jinks move into her house while theirs was repaired. It was pointed out that no decisions could be taken until after the meeting about a School Board in Reigate the next day.

Local builder Mr Bagaley had a look at the clock tower and at first refused to have anything to do with it, saying it was very dangerous, the stonework having crumbled away leaving the six-ton upper part supported only by 4½ inch brickwork.

It was proposed that Mr Bagaley be empowered to pull the tower down. Either Mr Hesketh had a word with him or Mr Bagaley independently modified his opinion for he later said it was not so bad as he had first thought, and submitted an estimate for repairs to the July 1882 meeting. Unfortunately this coincided with the announcement by Mr Bourne that if all outstanding accounts bar one were paid the school funds would be exhausted. The one account left being £25 owed to the churchyard fund. This statement does not support the claim of February that £951 was in hand for enlargement.

At this time (July 1882) a letter was written to Canon Cazenove, a prominent Reigate cleric, stating that the Managers of St John's were very anxious to avoid a School Board and felt that the only way to avoid it was to establish a voluntary rate for the whole Parish, including nonconformist as well as Church Schools. The letter urged Canon Cazenove to join with Mr Adeney, the leading dissenting minister in the Parish, in calling a meeting accordingly. The letter ended by saying that this ought to be done without delay or a School Board would be upon them before they knew it.

Part of the old St John's School building after enlargement in 1861. The clock in the existing tower is dated 1861 and all the evidence points to it being the original as installed at this date. These buildings were among those demolished and replaced by the current upper school building in 1910.

The Rev. Gosse Retires 1882

The Rev. Gosse had now been the vicar of St John's Church for thirty-eight years and earlier in 1882 had indicated that he was thinking of retiring. Later that year he did indeed retire, his place as vicar of St John's being taken by the Rev. J.M.Gordon.

Perhaps he would have stayed longer as vicar but for increasing deafness, although he remained at the Parsonage which he later renamed 'The Firs' and helped out at the church whenever asked. (The 'Firs' stands at the north west corner of the crossroads by Mill Street and Brighton Road. It has a Regency canopy on its lower front and was built originally as a coaching inn called 'the Somers Arms'. It ceased in this capacity when the railways brought an end to the coaching traffic in the 1840s. It became St John's Church vicarage and later the private residence of the Rev. Gosse, who apparently gave it its name).

The Rev. Gosse resigned the Chair of the Management Committee at the July 1882 meeting and the Rev J.M.Gordon took over. One of the new Chairman's first tasks was to propose that the United School Committees (St John's and St Matthew's) had a meeting before a Reigate one at which the Bishop of Rochester was going to be present, and which no doubt dealt with that old chestnut, School Boards.

Repair or Enlarge? 1882 - 1883

In August 1882 three contractors, Messrs Bagaley, Peat and Room, tendered for repairs to the Master's house. The question of the best way to repair the clock tower was referred to Mr Hesketh. The raising of the necessary funds was put in abeyance until the Chairman had written to Mr Waterlow, a prominent local resident, to see if he would subscribe.

The matter of school enlargement came to a head in October 1882 when it was revealed that the population of the district was 4,200. The Government would require room for 700 children (one sixth of the population), 165 more places than were then being provided by St John's plus the two schools at Meadvale. Mr Paine said he thought the money would be impossible to raise especially because, at the rate of population increase, another enlargement would be required within a further few years, a view to which the rest of the Committee concurred. Nevertheless School Inspector Mr French was to be asked to prepare an estimate of enlargement cost.

In November 1882 the lowest estimate for the repairs to the Master's house, that of Mr Bagaley at £218, was accepted. His bill for £78 for repairs to the Boys' School and the tower was to be paid. Unfortunately Mr Hesketh had not realised that there was no interior brick wall to the Master's house and provision of this raised the cost beyond that which the Managers were prepared to consider at that stage. Incidentally, once again a motion was passed that meetings should be held monthly. In spite of this there were no meetings in December 1882 or January 1883. It is as if the resolutions had the opposite meaning to the words they contained.

The School on the Common

An Article in the Surrey Mirror of December 9th 1882 reported on a public meeting at which a committee had been appointed to consider whether funds could be raised to support the voluntary schools as they were or whether a School Board should be set up. The latter option would involve the levying of a rate on the whole Borough, it said, and would mean the disestablishment of religion in the schools and conflict with the church. The newspaper decided that, on the face of it, it would seem that the public support of all schools would be a good thing compared with the support of the schools by a few private individuals while the rest escaped scott-free. Statistics showed that the cost of educating each child in the Borough was £1.3.6 (per annum, presumably) whereas the cost of educating a child in London was £2.17.6.

This meeting was followed in late March 1883 by another meeting of the Managers of local elementary schools at Warwick Hall, Redhill, to take into consideration the school accommodation in the Borough. Mayor Alderman Field presided. Representing St John's were the Rev. J.M.Gordon, J.O.Gooch, R.L.Hesketh, William Oram, G.G.Stone, E.G.Field and Henry Bourne.

Her Majesty's Inspector of Schools said that the school accommodation in various parts of the Borough had been very defective and fell far short of requirements, and that steps needed to be taken to rectify matters. There was a large amount of accommodation but much of it needed considerable repair. Also other schools were wanted. The choice was between a School Board and raising the required funds:

St Luke's district (South Park)	£1000
St Johns	£2000 (£951 so far raised)
St Matthews	£3500 (£1500 so far raised)

There were several important schools in the district besides the church schools. Mr Duncan of Reigate School was invited to speak and said that Redhill were in favour of a School Board and the present was a very good time to inaugurate one. He thought that religious education would be continued under a School Board and the church school leaders should have no worries on the matter. He added that however Reigate schools tried to raise money for their schools they would not stave off the eventual coming of a School Board.

Budget Crisis 1883

In February 1883 St John's funds in hand had dropped to £50. The Managers wrote to the secretary of the Reigate Committee formed to look at school expenditure saying that they were unanimous that their only course of action was to give notice to the Department of Education that they would have to close the Schools. This sounds bad but at the same meeting the Managers increased the pay of the Master by £10 per annum as from the previous November, not the action of a totally doom-laden Committee. The result of the letter and a meeting with Mr Freshfield, the Reigate Committee Chairman, was that the Managers were urged to keep the Schools open until such time as the Reigate Committee could raise the money required for enlargement. In the meantime they would help with expenses. The Managers then wrote to the subscribers and others interested in the Schools and received promises of donations in the sum of £669. Again, no mention was made of any monies (especially £951) already held.

Vote to Keep Voluntary Schools 1883

The Surrey Mirror of 19th May 1883 reported on a public meeting on Schools at which the Market Hall was filled for its largest ever gathering. Presiding was the Mayor, Mr R.Field. The Meeting voted to keep the voluntary schools. St Matthew's Committee met separately and decided to provide its own school.

Funds at Last 1883

In the July of 1883 Mr Bourne, the Treasurer, resigned because he felt he had not been sufficiently consulted about the management of the Schools and he disapproved of the conduct of the services there. His resignation was accepted and the Rev. Gordon took over from him for the time being. The school account at this time was overdrawn by £80 and an overdraft facility of £150 was arranged.

The approach to the Reigate committee paid off handsomely. In October 1883 a letter was received by the St John's Managers to the effect that £1,500 had been promised as a result of a door-to-door canvass in Reigate. As a result Mr Haughton, an architect who had recently built a school at East Grinstead, was approached to advise about enlargement at St John's. He advocated splitting the current buildings into Girls' and Infants' Schools only at a cost of £300 and erecting a new Boys' School at a cost of around £4.10.0 to £5 per child.

Suddenly things looked much rosier, even to the point where the current year's expenditure had exceeded the income by only £9. The Managers decided to enlarge the Committee as well as the school. They held a meeting among the Subscribers that endorsed the collecting of the Reigate money and proceeding with the proposed enlargement. Plans were requested and approved and a Building Committee was formed with a number of outside people joining it. An assistant mistress, Miss A.Havitt, was engaged to look after the younger boys and girls at St John's during the changeover. The current Assistant Master seems to be the only disappointed person as the

Left is Annie Peat, Pupil Teacher at St Johns from 1880 to 1885. After she left St John's she went to be a teacher at the Diocesan College at Truro, rising to become College Head. The picture below shows her (seated) with some of her pupils, circa 1920s

The right hand picture once belonged to Annie Peat and may date from her time at St John's, in which case it is from 1880-85. It certainly dates from before 1895, by when the church spire had been rebuilt. All pictures reproduced courtesy Mrs B.D. Abrahams, all rights reserved.

committee refused his request for a salary increase quoting the unsettled times as a reason. He was replaced by a trained Assistant Master at Christmas.

The New Boys' School 1884 - 1897

The new Boys' School was duly built. It occupied a position nearer to Union Road (now Pendleton Road) and lower down the slope than the old original buildings, a position it still occupies. Today it houses a nursery school, one classroom from the upper school, and the hall doubles as gym and children's dining hall. Back in 1884 the boys had this brand new premises to themselves and those parts of the older buildings vacated by them were converted for just girls and infants. The opening of the new lower Boys' School must have occurred fairly late in 1884, probably at the end of October (the dedication of a new honours board on October 30th 1934 probably commemorated the 50th anniversary). A factor must have been that the ground it occupied was common land, and some arrangements must have been made to allow its construction there, unless somehow covered by the original 1840 appropriation of the land.

Above - the 1884 arch over the entrance to the lower building. As can be seen from the modern picture below the gas lamp has been removed and it is today adorned by conduit and cabling.

Strangely the construction and opening is not mentioned in committee minutes. Nor can we read about it in the Boys' School own logbooks for they only exist from 1885. These show that the staff then consisted of Mr Jinks, Master, with assistants Alfred Legg, E.J.Dewdney, Miss A.Hewett and Miss A.Peat. Mr Legg had started only that year, Miss Peat left at its end, and the Rev. Gordon started chemistry lessons at his house for standard VI and VII

boys. This was the same year that locks were first fitted to the boys' WCs; when pupil A.Jennings was expelled for stealing a little boy's dinner, and when two boys were readmilled (sic) for absences of two months. Also a new gate had to be fitted to prevent sheep, turned out on the common to graze, eating the shrubs at the front of the school.

New to the Boys' School in 1886 were teacher Walter Ansell and Pupil Teacher Robert Hewett. Mr Jinks had occasion to punish pupils Thomas Willett for swearing and Walter Shore for using filthy language. What the difference was is not recorded.

In 1887 the school was closed in March by Drs Ewen and Berridge for the old enemy of diphtheria. The method of controlling infection in the classrooms was the sprinkling of carbolic acid in the offices and its vaporisation in the classrooms. To make up some of the time lost the Whitsun holiday was cancelled.

A boy reported missing was found to have wandered to Brighton (quite a wander) and had fallen into the hands of the police. He was found in the Brighton workhouse and returned to his family. One day in June of that year was surprisingly different, for the boys, instead of having scripture lessons went for a march - not a walk or a stroll but a march - on the common. This may or may not reflect some sort of disciplinary standard at work but was better treatment than the unfortunate William Withers received; he was caught cheating in an exam and caned before the whole school.

Also in 1887 experimental extra-curricula Saturday morning classes were started for better-class children (educating the more able or just the more fortunate?) and in 1890

ST. JOHN THE EVANGELIST, REDHILL

ST JOHN'S NATIONAL SCHOOLS

FROM 1st JUNE, 1874, TO 31st MAY, 1875

COMMITTEE

REV. H. GOSSE, Chairman

Mr. BRISCOE	Mr. W. ORAM
Mr. HESKETH	Capt. RAMSAY
Capt. MARRYAT	Mr. G. G. STONE
Mr. W. D. PAINE	Rev. W. COOPER Secretary

REPORT, 1875

In presenting to the their Report for the past year to the Subscribers of the St John's National Schools, the Committee are thankful to be able to lay before them a satisfactory Statement, not only as to the efficiency of the Schools but also as to the amount of the Government Grant for the year, which is £180 4s 0d as against £152 1s 0d in the previous year.

The balance against the School has been reduced by about £35 and now stands at £60. They must, however, remark that the pecuniary gain will not be so great as it appears, because with the grant is coupled an intimation, for the second time, that the desks of the Boys' School ought to be renewed. Non-compliance with this would probably cause a deduction from the next year's grant.

The late Pupil Teacher F.Francis, with the consent of the Managers, resigned, his place has been supplied by a transfer from another school.

Several children were examined this year in Drawing for the first time, and have satisfied the requirements of the Science and Art Department fairly well. The grant earned was £3 19s 0d.

The Committee cannot close their report without allusion to the death of the late Mrs Price, who defrayed the cost of building the Boys' School and the Master's house, and has ever been a steady supporter of the Schools.

THE REPORT OF THE GOVERNMENT INSPECTOR

Boys' School.- "The Boys' School continues to improve. The general result of the examination in the standards very creditable. Geography and History less successful. The boys are under strict discipline, and are much more orderly, attentive and cleanly than they used to be. The exercises in drawing are full of promise. New desks are greatly wanted."

Girls' School.- "The Girls' School has progressed considerably since last year, examination as a whole satisfactory. The Geography was well answered. The repetition was very nicely said. The Needlework remarkably good, specimens of all sorts, cutting-out included, highly creditable. There is still extraordinary irregularity in the attendance. The numerous ink stains on the floor are to be regretted, giving as they do an air of untidiness to the school generally. Ink wells of a better sort, and greater care in filling them, would be desirable."

The Managers 1875 report. Ink stains on the floors must have been a great problem in the days of unsealed wood floors. Note reference to Mrs Price.

French and elementary science were introduced at evening classes but lasted only two years when classes were terminated through lack of numbers.

It is interesting to note a remark made at the prize giving of December 1887 by the Committee Chairman, the Rev. J.M.Gordon. He bid the children to do their best to successfully compete with, *'the deluge of foreigners who came to our country to fill up the places which really belong to our own boys'* (Surrey Mirror report of prize-giving of December 1887). The background to the remark is unknown.

As stated elsewhere, the grant was dependent on attendance, so log references to absent children frequently occur. In one seven-month period in 1891/2 one thousand absence enquiry forms were sent to parents. Enquiries about absenteeism in 1888 revealed that boys were employed by working mothers in 'minding the baby' or 'fetching the washing'. Earning enough to keep food on the table had to come before schooling.

ST. JOHN THE EVANGELIST, REDHILL

ST JOHN'S NATIONAL SCHOOLS

FROM 1st JUNE, 1875, TO 31st MAY, 1876

COMMITTEE
REV. H. GOSSE, Chairman

Mr. BRISCOE	Mr. W. ORAM
Mr. HESKETH	Capt. RAMSAY
Capt. MARRYAT	Mr. G. G. STONE
Mr. W. D. PAINE	Rev. W. COOPER *Secretary*

————————0000000————————

REPORT, 1876

In presenting to the Subscribers the Annual Report, the Managers have pleasure in calling attention to the continued efficiency and prosperity of the Schools. The Government Grant earned during the past year is £187, the largest amount ever received.

The balance against the Schools has been further reduced by about £20, and now stands at less than £40; special donations against clearing this off will be gladly received. It is also very important that the Subscriptions should be well maintained, as, over and above the ordinary expenses, more than £50 must be paid this year for work connected with the drainage of the Schools which has been entirely re-arranged at the insistence of the Town Council.

New desks have been provided for the Boys' School at a cost of £33 2s., specially contributed; and at the same time the Desks in the Girls' School have been improved. In this way the imperative requirements of the Government have been satisfied.

In the hope of encouraging greater regularity of attendance the Managers have this year given money prizes and medals to the most regular among the children.

Miss Denner resigned at Christmas the post of infant Mistress; her successor is Miss Scott.

Mr and Mrs Janney having sent in their resignation, their place will be supplied at Michaelmas by Mr and Mrs Jinks, who presented satisfactory credentials.

THE REPORT OF THE GOVERNMENT INSPECTOR

Boys' School.- "The Boys' School is in good condition. Examination very creditable, as well as in the elementary subjects as in Grammar and Geography. Discipline again very much improved. Recitation fluent and fairly intelligent. The attendance is increasing but still very irregular. The walls want paint and whitewash."

Girls' School.- "The Girls' School is in a fairly satisfactory state of efficiency, all circumstances considered. Examinations in the standards on the whole pretty creditable; but there are backward scholars in Arithmetic, especially in the upper standards, and the reading and recitation are rather too rapid and wanting in intelligence. The Geography is barely good enough to warrant a grant. The Needlework is very good, both the work exhibited and that done under examination. Discipline is strictly administered. The room is much tidier than it used to be. The scanty attendance of Girls as compared with Boys is to be remarked."

The Managers' report of 1876, in which the main drainage of the School and the arrival of the Jinks is mentioned.

Those who did attend were not always as well behaved as they might have been. One boy was admitted with grave reservations as at his previous school he had thrown a slate at a female teacher and punched her in the face. Others boys who were caught scrumping from a garden next to the school were made to apologise to the owner. They made up for this by returning to steal some of the apples they had left behind the first time. And Albert Betchley, in 1891, refused to hold out his hand for the cane. Upon being ordered to his classroom to receive punishment for insubordination he took up his cap and ran away through the front door. His mother, who had apparently made trouble on other occasions, turned up at the premises a little later and *'shouted out a deal of vile and filthy language.'* A pane of glass in the school was broken in 1893 by stone-throwing boys who finished up in court for the offence, the head taking a half-day to attend the case.

In 1892 the 'Penny Bank' savings scheme was started in the Boys' School. Club Cards, probably a similar savings scheme, had already been issued in the Girls' School annually, Miss Ramsay issuing them at least since 1886. In 1901 there is another reference to a 'Penny Club' in the Girls' School, probably the same or similar savings club aimed at encouraging thrift in children. No doubt such schemes fell into abeyance from time to time, as a new Penny Savings Bank was

ST. JOHN THE EVANGELIST, REDHILL

ST JOHN'S NATIONAL SCHOOLS

FROM 1st JUNE, 1876, TO 31st MAY, 1877

COMMITTEE

REV. H. GOSSE, Chairman

Mr. BRISCOE	Mr. W. ORAM
Mr. HESKETH	Capt. RAMSAY
Capt. MARRYAT	Mr. G. G. STONE
Mr. W. D. PAINE	Rev. W. COOPER *Secretary*

REPORT, 1877

In presenting to the Subscribers the Annual Report, The Managers have pleasure in stating that the Schools continue efficient and prosperous. The Government Grant for 1876-7, is £203.11s. against £187 for 1875-6. On the other hand, the heavy expenses in connection with the drainage and the sums laid out in painting, whitewashing, and repair of Buildings, have increased the balance against the School from £39 14s. 4d. to £86 9s. 6d., in addition to which £47 9s. has to be paid for repairs. Funds are therefore greatly needed.

The increased pressure brought to bear on parents, hitherto negligent, has caused an improvement in the attendance, but much still remains to be effected by an earnest co-operation with the Attendance Committee of the Borough of Reigate.

The School Treat will be given shortly after the re-assembling of the children, and Prizes and Medals will again be awarded to the most regular. The first Certificate of Honour, under the Education Act, has been gained by ALBERT ROOM, who will now be entitled to free education for three years, the School Fees being paid by Government.

Mr. and Mrs. JINKS succeeded last Michaelmas to the charge of the Boys' and Girls' Schools, and all three departments, Boys', Girls' and Infants', are now in good working order.

Mr. PAINE having last August resigned the office of Treasurer, received the cordial thanks of the Managers for his kind and efficient services, and the liberality he has shewn during many years. The present Treasurer is Capt. Marryat, R.N., Earlswood Common, Redhill, to whose 'order' Cheques should be payable, and crossed London and County Bank, Redhill.

Collector, Mr. JAMES GEAR, who will give a printed receipt for all monies collected.

The Managers' 1877 report. The Jinks arrived at Michaelmas, an old accounting period usually situated at the end of September each year.

begun in the Girls' School in January 1939.

Boys belonging to the choir were able to get out of school on Ascension Day each year (the school did not close for Ascension Day then) and on other occasions when the choir was needed to augment services in the church.

May 23rd 1895 saw many boys absent assisting at 'golf' on the common. The golf club had been started in 1887 so this occasion may have been one of its early special events that required more caddies than usual. On May 13th 1904 an application was received from the Secretary and Steward of the Golf Club requesting twenty boys to act as caddies (perhaps a similar event to the 1895 one). Mr Jinks referred the matter to the Borough Education Committee who reacted by warning the parents against allowing their sons to be absent for this purpose and sending the Attendance Officer to the 'golf ground' to take the names of any who did attend. In the event there were none, so presumably the club got its caddies from elsewhere.

May 1895 also saw the Jinks' daughters, Katherine and Bertha, following their parents into the teaching profession and taking their Pupil Teachers' examinations. In October of 1895 Charles Rennie was awarded a scholarship to the Grammar School, the 4th from St John's that year. In a less academic incident of 1896 a Mrs Merrett complained that her son had been caned for smoking off school premises. What her complaint achieved is not recorded, but as this author was also once caned for off-school activities some sympathy for Merrett junior is felt.

The main hall of the Boys' School originally had no partitions and in October 1885 the provision of curtains between classes held in it was proposed. Three, sometimes four classes were being taught in the one large room. The children, when answering teachers' questions, *'must speak so low they could hardly be heard otherwise noise becomes overwhelming.'* Partitions were not used because the Managers did not want to erect anything that could not be removed when the hall was used for public meetings - clearly folding partitions were either unavailable or were an option that was not considered. It seems strange that the problem of noise interference when more than one class was using the hall of the new school building had not been anticipated at the design stage.

The fact that the new school was not large enough is borne out by the fact that in 1897 the Managers had to acknowledge that it was full and limit numbers to two hundred and eighty. Incredibly this was only three years after its completion (remember the 1882 management committee concurring with Mr Paine' view about the population increase?) and one class worked outside when weather allowed to relieve conditions inside. The Headmaster was instructed to refuse all further applications for admission until numbers had fallen to the school's limit, which was now reassessed at two hundred and fifty. At the time a pupil could walk all the way around the building without going outside the school boundary but the building was extended to the west wall in 1897 with the addition of a cloakroom.

The separation of classes in the main hall was something remedied after a new Diocesan Schools Grant was apportioned to schools in the Borough in 1898. Unfortunately St John's share per pupil seemed lower than that distributed to other schools, in one case 50% lower, and there was much protesting correspondence generated as a result (Management Committee minutes Dec 6th 1897). The money, when sufficient was received, was to be put towards several projects at St John's, including the erection of a movable partition in the Boys' School as desired by HM Inspector.

The partitions had not been erected by April of 1899. This is known because assistant master Mr Savill started at St John's on April 10th of that year but resigned on the 13th. His reasons were that he was having to teach standard VI when he had thought he would be teaching standards VI and VII; he was not allowed to inflict corporal punishment; and with more significance to partitions, did not have a separate classroom. Had he stayed he would still not have had a separate classroom by the end of the century.

Mead Vale School 1884 - 1891

The School at Mead Vale (as it was then written) was at 20 Somerset Road and was originally a separate school for boys and girls of that area. The St John's Committee took over the management of it as from January 1st 1884. Unfortunately HMI report for Mead Vale St John's School in January 1886 was very unsatisfactory which, *'for the sake of the Mistress it would be as well not to publish',* and about which the Chairman of the Management Committee pointed out, *'it was the first time the School had been examined by the Government Inspector.'* Even more unfortunately the 1887 report was also bad, leading to thoughts of making it an infants only school by bringing all the other children to St John's. When the 1888 report was also bad and the standard of teaching was criticised this course of action was put into effect. The children moved in 1889 but moved back again in 1891 when new Department of Education rules meant a great deal of money would have to be spent on alterations.

Chapter Three
The End of an Era

Queen Victoria's Jubilees 1887 and 1897

Queen Victoria came to the throne in 1837 and her fiftieth and sixtieth jubilees were celebrated with considerable gusto by the upper and middle classes, and to a lesser extent by those of smaller means but probably with equal enthusiasm. After all, the opportunity to have a good time did not present itself that often for many people, so they would have joined in those public celebrations wherever and whenever they could. In June 1887 St John's children were practicing a new Jubilee song. Tickets for the Golden Jubilee celebrations on Wednesday 21st June were given out and school dismissed until then. On that day 700 children - St John's, Meadvale and the Sunday Schools combined - marched to the top of the Brighton Road with flags and garlands of flowers. There a Jubilee Ode and the National Anthem were sung before the children joined the main body of an even larger procession and marched to Mount Field for tea and sports until 8pm. Children were so tired the next morning that school was closed until the afternoon. A flag won by girls in the Jubilee tug-of-war was displayed on 24th June in school.

Ten years later, in 1897, a tea for all schools was again held in a field, this time adjacent to Great Doods, almost opposite the Grammar School at Reigate. The weather was reported as being perfect. An aspect of both jubilees not directly connected with St John's was the tree planting on the top of Redhill Common; these clumps of trees have been seen and played amongst by children for over one hundred years.

Home Lessons

Home lessons were the 19th century equivalent of homework. They were not always well received at home for on 19th February 1890 Lilly Richards was *'sent home with home lessons, to which her mother objects, and did not return for a week'.* On the same date it was noted that *'Ellen Roffey's mother objects to home lessons'.* The reasons for the objections are not noted but often children were expected to do a considerable amount of domestic and outside work at home, especially in more rural areas, and home lessons would have interfered with this.

Strangely enough it is twenty years before home lessons are mentioned in the logs of the Boys' School, when on 22nd September 1910 a log entry announced, *'Home lessons started'.* They were compulsory for Standard VII and the top boys in Standards V and VI, and the term *'home-work'* is used alongside the *'home lessons'* phrase.

The Upper School 1884 - 1894

When the boys moved to the new lower building in 1884 the girls and infants had been able to occupy the space vacated and must have had plenty of room. Inevitably this did not last and, before ten years had passed, they were finding space rather cramped. In September 1893 Mrs Jinks recorded that the small size of the Girls' School classrooms was making work difficult. In April 1894 she wrote that Standard II worked in the main room as their classroom was not large enough for paperwork, and that other classes were also crowded.

In June 1894 an architect came to look at the Girls' School, and in September work altering

27

classrooms meant that the Girls' School remained closed one extra week after the school's four-week break. When they eventually returned there were only 25 desks in the classroom and the rest of the girls sat on benches. On 18th October new desks were received and some others repaired and additional lighting installed, although the new desks were not fixed in place until 5th November when the stove had been moved.

On 18th November 1895 there was excitement in school over the ruins of the nearby laundry *'burnt on Saturday night'.*

In 1889 work began on rebuilding St John's Church to a design by Mr John Pearson RA, the designer of Truro Cathedral. The work took six years, with the spire added last. Money for this huge undertaking must have been raised as it went along, for on 6th June 1895 articles made in school were sent to a bazaar in aid of the spire fund. This picture shows St John's Church at about this time with a house in its grounds and still without a spire. Picture courtesy John Millican.

Changing Times

A report of January 1887 said that the girls' classroom walls were dull without pictures to brighten them up. In September 1888 pictures and demonstration needlework cards were hung around the Girls' School, *'much brightening it up'.* The Infants' School received several pictures each year and further pictures are mentioned in the logbooks almost every each year from 1890 - 1921. It is not stated that they were for decoration, however, and could have been to do with needlework or other curriculum activity (the 27th October 1898 entry mentions them as being *'for the use of the Infants' School'*). No mention of brightening the Girls' School occurs again until 16th September 1902 when two pictures, *'St Mark's, Venice* and *Westminster Abbey* 'were bought by the children for 15/- in commemoration of the coronation of King Edward VI and Queen Alexandra, and October 7th 1902 when four framed groups of girls were hung on the walls. In October 1903 a gravure, *Kitchener's Homecoming*, that the children obtained by collecting Bovril tokens, joined them.

In 1897 the school managers were reflecting on the changes that had taken place over the past few years. They remembered the times when the Schools were very small, when fees were paid and attendance was not so compulsory, and noted that bibles costing 3s 8d had been given to children leaving with good records and as an encouragement to others for good attendance. Now bibles cost 5/- and were given to children from well-to-do families who took advantage of free education in the enlarged school with its compulsory attendance without contributing to the school funds at all. A vote that the practice should be discontinued was carried by four votes to three, although it was agreed to give the bibles that year. In spite of the vote, Bibles were given for a few years after this.

Non-Attendance in the 19th Century

The importance of school attendance has been mentioned from time to time in the foregoing. Some of the reasons for non-attendance have been touched upon already but such were the varieties of reasons that before moving on to the 20th century, when attendance improved steadily, it is worthwhile completing the subject here and now.

Holidays - The main breaks were in the summer and winter as now, although there is no mention of half-term closures. The Schools closed for four weeks 20th July to 20th August (approx. depending on calendar). In the winter the school closed for two weeks around Christmas. The Attendance Officer called regularly at St John's and presumably most, if not all, other schools. He took the names of absentees and visited the homes of children with irregular attendance records. There seemed to be a habit for children to stop away on Friday afternoons, prompting a warning in April 1888. In October 1889 two mothers, Mrs Streeter and Mrs Whitmore, called at the school to complain that they had been summoned for the irregularity of their children. The cause of their complaint might have in part have had something to do with the inconvenience they faced, for court cases were held only at Reigate, and in the 1880s there was unsuccessful agitation for cases to be heard in Redhill as well. One of the reasons put forward as to why this should be adopted was that Redhill women summoned for education offences (such as irregular attendance) not only had to travel further to Reigate with their children but frequently had to wait all day for their case to be heard.

Treats, Excursions and Other Activities - Attendance was affected much more by local events than it is today, with children being given time off for many of them. On Ascension Day, 3rd June 1886, children who asked were given leave to go the games at the Philanthropic Farm School, and these occurred in several years. Attendance was much reduced only a month later, on 7th July, by the Wesleyan and several other schools excursion to Folkestone, Brighton, Eastbourne, Hastings and other coastal resorts. Sometimes half-holidays were given for events, such as on 8th July 1886 for the Foresters Fete. On 15th September of that same year so many girls asked for leave to go to the harvest festival at the Farm School that the registers were not marked in the afternoon. Some events, especially when there were two or more on one day, closed the school completely; at other times the attendance was just reduced by twenty or thirty children. A list of some of the regular events limiting attendance is given at the end of this chapter. (See also *Other Items of Interest.)*

Weather - Non-attendance was also due to children almost always having to walk to school and therefore being exposed to the elements. In times when medical attention was not always available, and when more fatalities occurred from chills and infections than today, children did not set out for school so readily in bad weather because sitting in school for half a day in wet clothes could lead to illness. When the weather was bad the school might be closed for a half day so that children did not have to get wet coming back in the afternoon.

In the summer of 1886 the Head Mistress, Mrs Emily Jinks, was attributing low attendance to the 'trying heat' and noting that on 1st September it was so hot that *'several girls noses bled'.* On 9th September 1889 it was so hot that younger children had to be given a half day.

Snow often closed the school, sometimes earlier or later in the season than we might expect, as it did for the days of 28th November 1890 and 25th March 1898 when school closed due to blizzards. On 10th and 11th March 1891 school was closed for two days due to bad weather, in fact the weather was so bad all week that half fees were charged the following week for those who attended at all. The weather on the following 9th March 1892 is recorded as snow and sleet once again. Preceding that blizzard of March 1898, high NE winds blew smoke and flame from the lower room stove into 'the room' (presumably the main hall) causing so much discomfort that school was closed at 4 o'clock.

Health - Although the majority of the health problems related to the children it was only because there were many more of them, so it ought to be noted that teachers got sick too, sometimes being off for several weeks at a time, other times returning only to have relapses. Associating as they did with so many children they may have developed some resistance to infections but at the same time they were putting themselves in contact with whatever infections were about.

Children were sent home from time to time because they had 'dirty heads' (a reference to lice), and to have them cleaned. Sometimes children were just 'spoken to' on the matter.

Disinfecting of school premises was often necessary after outbreaks of infectious diseases and this was done by burning sulphur. An additional precaution was the whitewashing of walls so they could then be more easily kept clean, and the washing of floors with carbolic acid (other methods are detailed elsewhere). This was certainly done at Meadvale School, possibly more than once, but the first mention of this being done at St John's is recorded in the Management Committee logs of December 1899 after the school had been closed for four weeks on advice from Dr Jacobs, the Borough Doctor. The cost was £31 and if borne by the school came at a time when the accounts were again just in deficit.

A class from c1884, the earliest known picture of children at St John's reproduced courtesy of Mrs B D Abrahams - all rights reserved.

Other Absences - In March 1887 it was recorded that absences were in part due to the inability of some families to pay the school fees. Sometimes there were prolonged absences that are not explained. Amelia Wickens, absent for more than a year, was re-admitted in February 1889. Margaret and Ruth Elliott arrived at school at 9.45am, a month after the 1889 summer holidays had ended, and were sent home as a consequence. They did not return.

Lateness - This was also a problem. In September 1890 the doors were locked each morning after prayers and each afternoon after Grace, a measure which improved lateness in most cases. Mrs Whitmore, however, resolved her children's habitual lateness by sending them to a different school. On 3rd July 1894 a girl was sent home, again after being late, an action the logs note as having '*a good effect upon lateness*'.

Calendar of Annual Local Events for which time was given off school:

January	Wesleyan Christmas treat - Infants' School treat - Earlswood Chapel School treat.
May 1st	'Maying' ('Maypoling' in the Boys' School logs) every year up to 1896.
May	Farm School sports and entertainment.
June-August	Multiple excursions to the coast by dissenting Sunday Schools, School Unions and temperance groups. Three Sunday School treats on one day in 1899.
June	Epsom races most years but in 1899 Derby Day '*did not*' affect attendance.

July	Baptist treat to White Hills 1888 - Earlswood Asylum festival every year - School treat at Earlswood 1891 - Temperance Band of Hope Sports - Water Fete or Aquatic Show by Earlswood Swimming Club 1893-94 - Flower show every year, either at 'The Mount' or at 'High Trees' - Band contest at 'High Trees' 1896 - Foresters fete every year.
August	Meadvale School treat 1889.
September	Farm School Harvest Thanksgiving every year - Visit of menagerie to the town 1887, 1888.
June-October	Circus on common twice a year every year usually resulted in half-holiday.
November	Preparations on the common for bonfire night and/or torchlight procession 1891-92-94.

In addition to the above many children went away to Kent picking hops in the school holidays and often did not return until October, and boys frequently missed school through helping in the fields at harvest time. If those listed were not enough regular reasons to miss school then there were quite a few extra reasons that cropped up over the years, such as military triumphs, royal anniversaries, coronations and visits, unusual local events and funerals of local dignitaries. Some may be dealt with in the main text but a list follows here.

1887 March 10th	Col. Pains, a former manager and treasurer of the school, was buried at St John's churchyard. The school was drawn up to witness his military funeral.
1887 June 10th	Queen Victoria's golden jubilee.
1888 April	Sunday School children and teachers gathering primroses to send to London.
1889 February 14th	School closed so teachers could go to funeral of School Inspector George French who died on 10th February.
1890 June 12th	The Rev. and Mrs Gosse gave a tea to mark their golden wedding. A china vase was filled with flowers and sent to their house from the Boys' School. The whole school assembled at 2.30, marched to The Firs on the corner of the Brighton Road and Mill Street where they cheered the Rev. and Mrs Gosse. They then went to the Mount Field lent by Mr Waterlow, for tea, cakes, bread and butter followed by the town band, balloons etc. until 8pm. (Presumably the field was adjacent to the house, The Mount, which stood about a quarter of a mile south of, and on the same side of Pendleton road, as St John's School) Only two years before, on 28th May 1888, the death of Miss Gosse, daughter of the Rev. and Mrs Gosse had occurred.
1892 July 8th	Polling day (other years the school was also required for elections).
1893 July 6th	Wedding of Duke of York and Princess May of Teck. School marched to High Trees for tea and entertainment (High Trees was a large house and seat of Mr Waterlow at the end of the present High Trees Road. It is now part of Dunnotar School). 'Day intensely hot'. Next day tickets and medals were sent to girls who were unable to attend because of measles.

The School on the Common

1896 April 27th	Holiday in afternoon to allow three teachers to be confirmed.
1897 June	School closed for week of 20-25th for Queen Victoria's Diamond Jubilee.
1898 June 8th	Attractive wedding at Reigate took many girls away.
1899 April 19th	Half holiday due to Earlswood Wesleyan Chapel foundation stone laid.
1899 June 30th	Duke of Connaught's visit to Farm School took a lot of children away.
1900 March 1st	The whole school was informed of relief of Ladysmith and the logs report that there was great excitement among the girls and boys, although no holiday being given is recorded.
1900 May 24th	Queen's Birthday and Relief of Mafeking - holiday given.
1901 January 30th	A half-holiday given for proclamation of King Edward by the Mayor.
1902 June 2nd	Peace had been declared in the Boer War on the Sunday night and some children arrived late at school after all night celebrations.
1902 June 6th	Sergeant Major Garton, for 18 years the Borough Attendance Officer, died. His funeral was held on the 10th and some children went.
1902 June	Coronation of King Edward, School closed one week (Decision by managers to close only after Mr Balfour announced that attendance would not be lost.) A planned tea at the school was thereby missed but the cake was brought in the following week on 30th June and distributed. Also, 20 copies of King Edward's Realm bought at 6d each as extra reader.
1902 September	Some girls attended a wedding at St John's Church on the 24th
1903	May 1st Local walking competition.
1903 May 7th	School closed p.m. for Rev. Gosse's funeral.
1903 June 18th	Very few present due to lady walking a ball through Redhill (see chapter four).
1903 June 30th	Poor attendance at school due to visit of General French to Farm School.

Details of absences for health reasons:

1887 March 14th	Girls' School - Ada Simmons died of diphtheria. Several others sick by same cause. Managers acting on Doctor's advice closed the school for two weeks.
1887 October 31st	Meadvale School closed due to fever and its girls refused admission to St John's.
1888 October	Emily Beales was kept from school because of mother's dread of diphtheria, which was again at Meadvale School. Mrs Jamman kept daughter Ellen at home for fear of diphtheria. Several deaths had occurred.

1889 January	Outbreak of measles.
1890 January	Influenza outbreak. 80 children off, school closed for 2 afternoons. Headmistress Mrs Jinks also caught it and was off for three weeks, the school being run by assistants only.
1890 September	Ringworm.
1891 March	Whooping cough and scarlet fever in Mill Street.
1891 June	Whooping cough and scarlet fever in Mill Street.
1892 October 26th	A standard V girl with diphtheria.
1893 February 3rd	Two or three cases of scarlet fever. The following week school closed for three weeks because three teachers ill. When school resumed Workhouse children plus some others prohibited from coming to school because of living near infected area.
1893 May 12th	Sickness in Mill Street and Workhouse. July - Measles among younger children.
1894 May 21st	Workhouse children off because of chickenpox.
1895 September	Closure of Infants' School for 2 weeks, no reason recorded.
1895 October 28th	Scarlet fever, 1 infant.
1895 November	Workhouse girls absent due to fever and several other cases in December when School closed until after Christmas by order of Sanitary Authority.
1896 September	School closed for 2 weeks by Sanitary Authority - fever case in Kings Alley.
1897 May 4	Fever case in Earlsbrook Road.
1897 November	Sister of fever case moved to fever hospital. School closed for 4 weeks because of scarlatina (scarlet fever).
1898 March 29th	E.Charman sent home, dirty head, already home for 5 weeks for this reason.
1898 April 19th	Re-opened after Easter, E.Charman again sent home, re-admitted Apr 29.
1898 August 27th	Infant with typhoid fever.
1898 August 29th	Absences with face eruption.
1898 September	One case of scarlet fever.
1898 October 6th	Another case of scarlet fever reported.

The School on the Common

1899 October	Infants' School - Edith Ware died of diphtheria.
1899 November	School closed 3 weeks by order of Sanitation Authority, then closed until after Christmas because of infectious illness (7 weeks altogether).
1900 May 10th	Diphtheria.
1900 May 11th	The Sanitary Inspector visited Infants and ordered William Shore, who was suffering from scarlatina, not to attend.
1901 January 21st	Workhouse children absent due to fever in house.
1901 February 11th	Ringworm.
1901 March 10th	Re-opened after 2 weeks closed by measles and flu.
1902 January	Re-opening of school delayed from January 6th to 18th because of measles and flu.
1902 October 8th	Workhouse children sent back due to diphtheria.
1902 November 7th	One girl in hospital with diphtheria.
1903 October 19th	Alice and Ethel Church absent, diphtheria in house.
1903 October 23rd	Lily Moody and Florence Feldwich absent, diphtheria in houses.

Adults and children gathered at St John's Church for what, judging by the canopy that reached all the way up to the church, must have been quite a fashionable event, although it might not have been the 1902 wedding referred to above.

Chapter Four
The Twentieth Century

Growth and Conditions 1900 - 1902

The turn of a century is often seen as a turning point in the affairs of people and institutions but in reality is only a point on the calendar like all other points. There was little that was different about the transition from the 19th century to the 20th at St John's other than it was marked by a longer than usual holiday owing to the closure of the school by the Sanitary Inspector from 21st November 1899 to 8th January 1900. One year later, however, there was real change with the death of Queen Victoria on 22nd January 1901, and the proclamation of King Edward VII on 30th January. Many local schoolchildren assembled in front of the Market Hall, Redhill, to hear the proclamation officially read out.

By the end of 1901, 176 participants in the Boys' School savings scheme collectively had £100 in the bank. Had they wanted to they could have paid for the partition that had still not been fitted. Mrs Jinks retired as head of the Girls' School at the end of 1902 after 25 years. Her husband remained at the Boys' School. At the time the total number on roll at St John's was 730.

Changes occurred at St John's with the arrival of the new Girls' Head Mistress, Miss Greening in 1902. The Girls' School logs start to record activities outside the school that varied from singing in the playground to local walks to Reigate Priory, Meadvale Copse, Earlswood Lakes and other places for the purpose of geographical and nature studies. Frequently they also took the forms of treats for girls with good attendance records. On 3rd October 1902, 130 girls visited a missionary exhibition in Reigate. In July 1903, 33 went to London for the day, seeing the Tower, St Paul's and the South Kensington Museum. It was a long day as they arrived at London Bridge at 9 a.m. and departed Victoria at 7.15 p.m. On June 11th 1904, 60 girls and eight adults visited zoological gardens. Visits such as these may have been undertaken before but in view of the total silence of previous logs on the matter it seems unlikely, and the arrival of the new Head Mistress seems to have been the start of a new era at the Girls' School. In the Boys' School too there started to be more trips out of a similar educational nature.

Another innovation was the receipt of items from private companies for use in the Girls' School. Often the goods were not named, logs merely saying, *'specimens received from Messrs Colman, and Bryant and May' (9th May 1902)*. On 16th May natural history pictures were specified as received from Messrs Colman. On 3rd October 1902 specimens of Bovril were received for use in the Domestic Economy lessons that were part of a course commenced in place of one on plant life, and on 12th November specimens were received from Tate and Lyle, presumably for the same course. These were followed by a case of coffee from Horrockses in December. In 1903 commercial travellers are mentioned for the first time, albeit in the Infants' logs. One was from 'Nelson's', one from 'Educational'.

Girls with full attendance were taken to Redhill on 2nd June 1902 to see the decorations. These were put up to celebrate peace declared following the Boer War and probably stayed up for the forthcoming coronation, as both occurred that June. Before the girls went to Redhill there was a ceremony that is best described by reproducing the report from the *Surrey Mirror*. -

'The receipt of the news at St John's Schools, Redhill was the occasion of a very impressive incident. At 11.30 on Monday morning the children were massed together on the open common in front of the school building, and the boys and girls departments each prettily rendered the Coronation Ode. There then rang out in the still summer air the sound of 600 shrill voices in the regular swing of the grand 'Old Hundredth' - 'All people that on earth do dwell'. The loyal little gathering dispersed after a hearty rendering of the National Anthem.'

The school closed for the Coronation from 23rd-27th June but none of the planned ceremonies were held as the King was ill and the Coronation delayed until later in the year. What could not be delayed was a cake that had already been baked and which was bought by the Coronation Festivities Committee. Whatever its form was - one cake or a number - 350lbs of it were delivered to St John's for distribution among the children.

In July 1902 the Boys' School finally got its partition. It was fitted in the centre of the main hall to divide it into two. By then there were over 300 on the register. In October a Borough Education Committee ruling reduced Pupil Teachers' hours to 17 per week, which did not help as their presence assisted greatly with the management and teaching of so many pupils.

The common was becoming more and more an extension of the school. When those selected girls had gone to see the decorations in Redhill the remainder had enjoyed games on the common. In July 1902, nets and balls had been bought and a tennis court laid out. The purpose was stated to be to bring together teachers and past and present pupils and to generally raise the tone and standing of the School. The tennis court was later installed inside the school perimeter where holes in the playground took net posts (also mentioned under heading 'Phyllis Cooper' at the end of the section on the 1920s).

1902 finished with the Girls' School being closed because the Head Mistress lodged in a house where diphtheria had broken out. Many boys also stayed away because of the scare.

Problems

At the same time as the 1902 change of Head in the Girls' School, Gertrude Franklin took over from Miss Spurway, who had been the Infants' Schoolmistress for 23 years. The new Mistress's log entries were much more comprehensive but her time there began badly with 70 infants off with measles or whooping cough in the February, and school closed for two weeks. By March, attendance was up to 154, but sending 61 children to the upper schools left 131 on roll. In the May, the aptly named May Williams was sent to private school as *'her father is so angry because there is always some illness at St John's School that he won't let her come again'*.

Problems continued in June, *'....the children from the Workhouse have been absent all week. It is quite hopeless of thinking of ever teaching them anything. They are always kept away and simply spoil the classes.'* (because they got so far behind the others), and in July, *'167 on roll. The room is most awkward to work in and the babies' class much too large, but there is nowhere else for them to go. During the last 2 weeks of hot weather the rooms have been simply poisonous and the children have been taught in the playground as much as possible. A new teacher is very greatly needed but it is no use to ask for one. The Pupil Teachers are each away two half days a week, which makes the work a great deal worse to arrange.'* (The Pupil Teachers were away two half days because of the previously mentioned reduction in their hours) By November things must have been even worse because there were 182 on the books and HMI Report for 1901-2 noted, *'There is every indication that increased accommodation will be required in this part of the town before very long.'*

Hurt by Name . . .

On 2nd March 1903 a teacher with the unusual name of Mr Hurt started in the Boys' School. On 18th March Mr Jinks had to intervene in an altercation between Mr Hurt and a boy in his class, and as a result had to tell Mr Hurt that he must not cane boys; this was to be left to the Head. Two days later Mr Hurt had caned 5 boys within 10 minutes of school opening, and a further flogging of a boy caused that lad to run home and be brought back by a complaining father. At the end of that day Mr Hurt was told that his services were no longer required. This apparently necessary departure of this teacher did not help the Boys' School situation, which had increased again to 324 on roll. The precise situation was as follows: -

Standard 0	24 boys	*no teacher*	
Standard I	55 boys	Miss Thirkettle	
Standard II	55 boys	Miss Pullen	
Standard III	55 boys	*no teacher*	
Standard IV	55 boys	*teacher advertised for*	
Standard V	50 boys	Mr Bath	
Standards VI & VII		30 boys	Mr Jinks

Mr Jinks had written to the Borough Education Committee but as there were no new staff available the remedy for the above situation had to be: -

Standard 1	69 boys	Miss Thirkettle and a monitor *	
Standard II	48 boys	Miss Pullen	
Standard V	52 boys	Mr Bath	
Standard III – VII		141 boys	Head and two Pupil Teachers **

* Monitors were youngsters paid 7s a month and normally employed for ringing the bell at break times, carrying supplies to classrooms, clearing up outside and other such general duties.
** Pupil Teachers reduced to 17 hours per week each

The Leaving Age

At the beginning of the new century the school leaving age was raised from 13 to 14. This no doubt come as a blow to some families that had been depending on a son or daughter getting employment and beginning to bring some money home. A first there was a certain amount of confusion about the situation which particularly affected three girls who had been sent notice of leaving in May 1901 as they had reached 13, but as the leaving age had risen to 14 the Attendance Officer had to be told of the circumstances. He is recorded as having called to discuss the situation but it is not recorded what he did about it. In September 1902, however, Mabel Styles was ordered to return to School as she was under 14, and in January 1903 he returned a girl of 13 years and nine months who had gone to service in Reigate.

New Infants' Mistress and Rules for Playground Supervision

Miss Franklin was succeeded in the Infants' School on 5th January 1903 by Edith M.Whyman. The new mistress was not impressed with writing standards and got each class to start again on this subject with 'Royal' copy books as the teacher's guide. On the 22nd January 1903 there was a new rule that two teachers must be present in the playground during playtimes. A log entry tells us that up to this time there had been no supervision at all. In February of 1903 Kindergarten (sic) games started as an inducement to better attendance, especially on Friday afternoons.

In May the school was closed for the Funeral of the Rev. Gosse, for so many years the vicar of St John's and chairman of the Management Committee.

The advantage of extra room for the infants created by the Boys' School getting separate own premises in 1884 had, by 1903, been lost by rising numbers. Log entries of July reflected - *'Babies much happier in classroom, but four classes working in the main room is not conducive to quietness'*. And another entry in August - *'We have now 198 children on books and all the classes are terribly overcrowded. Good work is impossible while we suffer from lack of room and an insufficient staff'*.

In June 1903 the children were allowed to go to Redhill to see a woman walking to Brighton on a ball. Mlle Florence walked a ball from London to Brighton in six days for a bet.

The Threat of a School Board Becomes Reality in 1903

Although St John's School never had a School Board imposed upon it the 1902 Education Act swept away School Boards and transferred responsibility to Educational Councils with more comprehensive powers. Local authorities were empowered to set up education committees, and early in 1903 Reigate Council decided to adopt these powers. It bought the two teacher's houses on the site for £600 and, under the provision of the Board of Education Act of 1899, and the Board of Education (Powers) Orders in Council 1900-1902, took over from the Church of England the Girls' and Infants' Schools for a nominal payment (not specified), paying the costs of all transfers in addition.

The Education Committee was to consist of a Council-appointed Chairman with local school managers invited to become members. The Rev. J M Gordon, Vicar of St John's, still checked the registers regularly. Also the Attendance Officer called as before to collect names of irregular and absent children, and the Diocesan Inspector still annually tested the children on their religious knowledge. The move to a single authority was the beginning of a long period of local government administered education in the Borough of Reigate.

To try to overcome her staffing problems the Infants' Mistress wrote to the Borough Education Committee asking for a certificated teacher saying that she found it impossible to do really efficient work with the staff she had. The classes were small but very backward, she said, and she could not make them larger on account of the room and want of seating accommodation.

Accommodation was also wanting as there was no gas lighting in the cloakroom so school had to finish earlier than usual at 3.40 p.m. on winter evenings so the children could find their clothes and get dressed before it got dark.

Prize-giving

The annual prize-giving up to now had been held each December, except for one or two occasions when School closed due to fever and prize-giving had been held in January. Only the older children were normally present. 'Standard' prizes were awarded by the teachers to those children who had gained the highest overall marks in the monthly exams. Needlework prizes in the form of workboxes were given to the girls by the ladies who had an interest in such work and came into the school year on year to oversee the needlework. Bibles were still presented to boys and girls leaving with good conduct records extending over three years in spite of previous management committee reservations on the matter. Monetary prizes of from 2/6d to 1/- were given to those with the best attendance records.

After 1884 prize-giving for the whole school seems to have been held in December in the new Boys' School. This continued until May 1903 when the prize-giving for the girls started separately in the Girls' School. In 1904 there is a mention of the Infants' prize-giving being in the morning, so it looks like the whole event had been re-arranged so more parents could attend.

Poor Conditions in the Upper School

If things were bad in the Infants' School then they were not good in the Girls' School either. Both had been closed for a week in November 1902 for the drains to be repaired and during January 1903 the large room in the Girls' School was very cold, another stove being needed. Partition glass in the Girls' School was whitewashed to prevent children looking through at adjacent classes.

In June a surveyor came to measure the upper building. In November the already inadequate stove was broken and the children were shaking with cold at 52 degrees F. An oil stove was brought in but a log entry soon recorded, *'Upper School bitterly cold, coal stove still broken and oil stove broken'.* The stove was repaired and good fires burned but the temperature was still 52 degrees, and in December was 47 degrees F. at 9 a.m. Then an entry records, *'Sulphur from stoves in Girls' School affecting teacher's voices'.* The 1903 Inspectors' report seems to understate the situation in saying, *'The school is overcrowded and teaching is carried on under difficulties. The lighting and ventilation are unsatisfactory.....'*

1904 began with the Infants' School staff list showing Miss Whyman for the first time as 'Head', and not 'Mistress' as always had been the case before. She had two assistants, two Pupil Teachers and 224 children. Wet playtimes must have proved very difficult. The 1904 Inspector's report again commented on the situation whereby 198 infants were crowded into accommodation intended for 146, adding that nothing seemed to have been done to amend the same situation reported the year before, a comment he was to repeat in 1905.

The Boys' School was also getting nowhere nearer reducing its overcrowding or getting extra staff. With 319 boys and only four adult staff plus the Headteacher things were as bad as ever. Repeated requests for extra staff over the past year had all been rejected. It had been nineteen years since the boys had moved into their new building and in all departments of St John's overcrowding was as bad as it had ever been.

On 17th June 1904 *'School closed at 11 am to allow the children to get into town to see the Buffalo Bill procession.'* This referred to Buffalo Bill Cody's 'Wild West' show that visited Redhill Sports Ground on that day. The procession was the advertisement for the main show, which included the attack on the Deadwood Stage, the passage of the Pony Express rider, the emigrant train and Indian fights. This was a time when local people lived with the horse every day yet it was reported at the time that those watching warmed not just to the entertainment and the reality of the events, which were popular with children and adults alike, but to the horsemanship of the riders.

The first annual sports for elementary schools was held at Redhill Sports Ground on 23rd July 1904. St John's girls won four 1st prizes, three 2nd prizes and four 3rd prizes. Silver cups were brought to the school the next day to be held for one year.

A Project and the Colman Institute

A 1904 project at the Girls' School was to write about the life of Lord Rosebery, and 21 of the girls involved got to see that gentleman in the flesh when he came to Redhill at the opening of the Colman Institute at the end of October that year. The Colman Institute was a working men's club that once stood on the town side of the Redhill Sports Ground, and the building of it was the idea of the then Mayor, Mr W Conolly, who had originally wanted to build a swimming baths on the site. This scheme had been modified to a working men's club when the entire money for it had been offered by Mr Jeremiah Colman of Gatton. Mr Crosfield of Reigate had offered to put up the money

The Brand new Colman Institute at Redhill from a sketch by Mr Hubert Gilford A.R.I.B.A. Courtesy Surrey Mirror

for the swimming pool but only if it was built in Reigate, not Redhill. (He eventually did fund a swimming baths at Reigate, which opened in 1906, and St John's children made good use of it.) Lord Rosebery, a prominent Liberal politician who was Prime Minister from 1904-6, came to Redhill to propose the vote of thanks to Mr Colman. A number of speeches were made and whilst replying to one speaker, and referring to the fall of Khartoum, Lord Rosebery was interrupted to his

Inside the Colman Institute at the ceremony attended by girls from St John's. Centre is Mayor Conolly; on his right is the donor of the Institute, Mr Colman; on his left is Lord Rosebery. Courtesy Surrey Mirror

expressed annoyance by someone shouting out, 'How about Gordon?', probably a reference to the dallying of the relief force and the murder of General Gordon on the palace steps at Khartoum. A policeman was dispatched to the rear of the hall to find out who the heckler was but failed to do so. It was a small incident that must have interrupted proceedings for some minutes.

Although the hall was crowded the St John's girls hopefully got in to witness the proceedings at first hand and be present at one of the major local events of the century. If they did not then they would presumably have only glimpsed the man himself as he passed them in his arriving motor car at 5 p.m. Their wait might have been a wet one as it rained heavily, and it would also have been quite dark by then. Coloured lights adorning a nearby stables and the Sultan public house might have added some cold comfort. It may have been that some contact was made with Mr Jeremiah Colman, for a week later he sent a specimen of a pitcher plant to the school.

More Incidents and Practical Work

As we have already discovered, some school log book entries tell of incidents but do not give us the whole story. One such Girls' School entry for 28th September 1904 reads, *'Mrs Withers came up to apologise for insulting Miss Watling in school during the dinner hour. Her husband did the same thing about a year ago.'* We can only wonder what led to the insults in the first place. A few days later a troublesome Florence Mew was sent from one class to another, *'to learn how to behave properly. Her sister forced her way into the main room and abused the Mistress during the afternoon.... Florence Mew rushed out of school. Her mother came up and created a disturbance.'* Florence returned the next day but, *'went home after being asked to apologise for her insolence....'* There are no more relevant entries, so we do not learn the final outcome.

Other entries tend to leave us with perhaps slightly the wrong impression. In November 1904, *'the vicar called* (at the Girls' School) *and stayed several minutes examining the nature study books.'* This makes one want to comment how good of him it was to spare the time but no doubt there was much more to the visit and such a comment would be unfair. The wording of some other enteries, although no doubt clear in the mind of the writer, leave the reader unclear as to their meaning. *'A Colonial Gentleman spent the afternoon watching the children at work.'* (4th November 1904) Who was he? Did he wander in off the street wearing a tropical suit and a safari helmet? *'The loud voices of the men when taking drill classes under the Girls' School windows are often most annoying and distracting.'* (7th September 1904) What men? If their voices were <u>often</u> annoying they must have been there frequently. Who were they? As stated elsewhere in this history the boys did drill (and the girls did too). Should we substitute 'boys' for 'men'. It seems that we shall never know.

Practical work for the girls took the form of knitting, hemming, darning socks and mending stockings (they brought their own in from home for the purpose) and needlework. The latter included making buttonholes in canvas and other coarse materials, run and fell seams in calico, and herring boning on flannel in preparation for run and seam in flannel. The girls were also reported as, *'making good progress in cutting out. They have well mastered the chemise in three sizes and are now practising a yoke to nightdress in three patterns.'* ('Run and fell' seams were seams completed by cutting away part of the pre-stitched seam, turning and stitching again to make it flatter and neater. 'Herring boning' was the stitching of a seam at two angles along its length – the method used by my grandmother when making my grandfather's flannel undershirts. AJM).

In other subjects, grammar and writing practice were taken twice a week and *'the practical working in arithmetic is found to be exceedingly slow. The reason for this has yet to be determined; it seems probable that there has been too much oral work and too little individual effort.'* This last log was written on 2nd October and quite possibly hit the mark, for on 3rd October: - *Miss Dawson has almost lost her voice, and to avoid straining will take Wednesday's lessons instead of Tuesday's as the latter are chiefly oral'.* And on 4th October: *'Miss Watling has almost lost her voice; her class will do knitting first lesson and composition after play.'*

Poor Conditions Due to Overcrowding and Other Causes

In May 1905 an Infants' School log stated *'This School is grossly overcrowded and no further admissions must take place without the express permission of the Board of Education'.* This was not the action needed but at least the infants' staff now knew where they stood and could arrange classes accordingly. In October another log recorded that not only could there be no relaxation of the no new infants' admissions rule but the first class would have to be retained there as Standard I as there was no room in the upper schools either. (The terms 'classes' and 'Standards' were both in use. The author assumes that a class was a group of children in a certain location, whereas a 'Standard' was a group of children being educated to a specific syllabus.)

Needless to say, parts of the Inspector's reports for the Infants' School continued to be critical. In 1905 he stated that, *'...very good work is being done in these badly lighted, badly arranged and in every way unsuitable premises.'* The thought arises that if they were bad as stated in 1905 then the only way they could have been better in the past was through being less crowded, so had otherwise always been bad. In some respects they had been worse because extra gas lighting had only recently been installed and since 1904 a spare room in the house at the school had been used as a classroom. Previously the room had also been used for medical inspections.

Mr Jinks, in the meantime (1904) was asking for a tap to be provided in the Boys' School playground as the only place the boys could get a drink was from the tap in the water closet room or from the water closets themselves. He was also writing to Dr Grece (Clerk to the Borough Education Committee and Town Clerk to the Borough of Reigate since its inception in 1863) on the subject of extra staff, and was still getting nowhere. One of the problems was that the Borough Education Committee was fixing salaries at the lowest end of the pay scale without any allowance for previous teaching experience, so were not attracting the staff needed. By 1905 the Schools Inspector, as in the Infants' School, fixed the maximum number on roll in the Boys' School at 270, and said that no further admissions were allowable while this figure was exceeded. Mr Jinks suggested that the Mission Rooms at Earlswood might be used for younger children. On 14th July there were plans for proposed alterations to the lower building.

The Girls' School situation was no different, a log of June 1905 stating, *'This school is much overcrowded and there should be no further admission without the express previous sanction of the Board of Education, so long as the number on the books exceeds 270. Signed: J C Colhill HMI.'*

Money, or the lack of it, was the root of the staffing problems, and of what might appear to be the lack of a school rebuilding programme. To understand why there was a shortage of money we can look at the capital expenditure of the Reigate Borough Council at this time. We see that the Municipal Buildings were erected in 1901-1902; the Borough's own electricity supply station was being built along with the network of cabling to supply the Borough with power, and Frenches Road School's foundation stone was laid in October of 1903. Several other schemes were under way, not the least of which was the widening of five local railway bridges, including Reading Arch and the tunnel under the station, a good part of the very substantial cost of which fell upon the Council. All of these required the Council to borrow money that had to be repaid from it's only income, the rates. High rates made for unpopular local government, so savings had to be made where they could and other highly necessary works postponed. The first mention of the intention to replace the old upper building, however, occurs in the 1906 logs of the Girls' School: - *'Mr Barnes, member of the Education Committee, called concerning the new building to be erected.'*

It was not only the overcrowding that caused discomfort in the old buildings but also the continuing cold in winter and excess heat and lack of ventilation in summer. A Girls' School log of July 1905, when inside temperatures reached 86°F, records how this latter was dealt with: *'At the end of each lesson the classes will lead into the playground and stand in lines ready to lead in again. This will ventilate the rooms and give the children change of position. The lessons must be made five minutes shorter.'* Hard to think that in January 1907 the thermometer stood at only 42°F inside at 9 am and 50°F at the end of the day, with the thermometer hanging two yards from a stove. Overcrowding was slightly alleviated by children having drill or other lessons outside in good weather, but was worsened by having to be crowded together inside during bad.

School closed for treats and circuses as usual and even closed one afternoon so that Mr A.Lund Newel, Secretary to the Borough Education Committee, could make a report on furniture and apparatus in the school, highlighting (if it needs to be highlighted this far into this history) that uninterrupted education seemed then not quite the priority it is today.

Sickness was even more prevalent among children and teachers throughout all departments of the school than before, with all the old illnesses recurring. In September 1905 teacher Miss Mudge had to give up her post in the Girls' School through having whooping cough. Miss Arnold started in the Girls' School on 12th February 1906 and resigned on 1st April because of illness at home. A pupil died of appendicitis in 1906 and in the same month a monitor from the Boys' School was rushed to the isolation hospital with diphtheria. One girl, Elsie Hewitt, was at school on 7th June 1907 and died of diphtheria on June 14th, Tom Hewett of the Boys' School having died only the day before of the same disease. On November 1st 1907 the whole school was closed by the Medical Officer of Health and did not re-open until January 6th 1908, nine weeks later. In spite of this another child, four years old Lewis Foster, died of diphtheria in October 1909.

Numbers in the Infants' School fell from 244 to 166 but most other things continued without improvement in 1906 and 1907. Staffing problems in the Girls' School eased somewhat, however, and a 1906 upbeat log entry recorded, *'It is so pleasing to note how punctual the Staff and children are. The assembly has been steadily improving through the year, and the children are just beginning to march with ease* (there's that drill again). *The constant changes of staff last year made it impossible to attain a high standard of efficiency in general work and discipline.'* The staffing problem was not helped when Miss Dawson, *'had a serious bicycle accident.'* She was off school for a month and on light duties upon her return.

Empire Days

Empire Day was celebrated annually at the Schools at least from 1903 (the first mention of it in the Infants' logs). It was a time of patriotic lessons about 'The Flag' and of dressing up in costumes of the various countries of the British Empire. In October 1904 a violin club of 20 girls and boys had been formed and it accompanied the singing on at least one of the Empire Day celebrations. The marching previously referred to was also used on Empire day, when, *'A flag was erected on the*

Empire Day 1909 and Mr Jinks stands firmly in control of the children paraded in the playground of the old school building

common and the schools assembled round, saluted it, and sang the National Anthem. The promptitude and Esprit de Corps were very pleasing, their marching in blocks was audibly commented upon by the spectators. The teachers had evidently taken great pains with the marching.' Where the flagpole and the flag were obtained is not recorded, but the following year the flagpole was donated by Mr E C P Hull and erected in the playground, and the flag provided by Mr Trevor Hull. The ceremony was similar to that of 1906 but there was no half-day holiday granted because the chairman of the Borough Education Committee was away and his permission could not be sought. It was also held later than usual on May 31st because the normal day coincided with the Whitsun Holiday.

In 1908 Empire Day was even more of a Hull family affair when (slightly puzzlingly) it is again mentioned that the flagpole was donated by Mr E C P Hull, the flag given by Mr Trevor Hull. It was raised by Miss Evelyn Hull. To add to the puzzle Mr Hull senior was reported by the Surrey Mirror as saying that they were there for the first time in the history of the Borough to celebrate Empire Day, which is untrue as we know from the log books. He also said that it was a great honour for St John's to be the first school in the Borough to own its own flag. On 9th November of that same year it was able again to be raised to mark the King's birthday. In 2003 a large, old Union Jack was

The assembled Girls' School on Empire Day 1911

Mr Hull lived close to the school at The Mount and was a prominent local figure and County Councillor. His initial P stood for Pendleton and was presumably the source of the name of the road next to the school that was renamed from Union Road around 1938 when the Workhouse was closed.

Empire day 1912

discovered in the loft at St John's and may have been this very flag.

On Empire Day 1911 Lily Mew represented Britannia in the celebrations in the girls' playground. The Mayor, Mr Lemon, and Mrs Lemon attended with Mr Lund Newell, the Borough Education Committee Secretary.

The Mayor and Mayoress of Reigate also visited on Empire Day every year from 1915 to 1918 and each year presented one or more pictures to the schools. A change occurred in 1919 when the celebrations were held in the afternoon and the Mayor and Mayoress are not recorded as having attended and no half-holiday was given. In 1920 a joint celebration with Hooley School was held on the common with the Mayor and his escort again in attendance. In 1921 and 1922 there were again joint celebrations with Hooley Mead Council School but were in the morning with a half-holiday. 1923 saw the celebration activities confined to St John's only in the school, where modern technology was employed when, *'Scholars heard gramophone record of King and Queen on Empire Day.'* This was followed by the usual half-holiday. 1924 Empire Day was a busy one, with the usual celebrations in the morning and the school sports in the afternoon, and in 1925 the children were once again on the common. Such arrangements continued through the following years (at least to 1938).

The common where the celebrations were held was alongside Mill Street, an unremarkable part of the common in the second half of the 20th Century but which had received some landscaping when it had been made into a 'pleasure ground' in the 1890s by the Commons Conservators. It became a favourite place for organised meetings of bands, temperance groups and religious organisations (and schools). Generations of St John's children remember it as the 'Flats', not to be confused with those even more level areas slightly nearer the school, the 'Lawns'.

Sport

One of the activities of many boys' schools in the country these days is football. Locally Reigate Priory FC was first registered in 1804 and Redhill FC was formed in 1894 and played at Wiggie for a number of years. At St John's Mr Jinks first spoke to the boys about forming a football club in the winter of 1899.

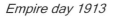

Empire day 1913

Presumably a team was got up at this time but it was not until 1904 that the Commons Conservators allotted space for a pitch on the common. The team entered the District Elementary Schools League that same year and were winners in 1911, just edging Cromwell Road by one point to take the Surrey Mirror Trophy for the first time.

Swimming was an activity new to the school from 1906 when the Reigate swimming baths were opened through the generosity of Reigate resident Mr J B Crosfield. The logs record that few boys could swim at all at first, then some began to get 25-yard certificates. On 4th October 1911, the same year as the football team won the Surrey Mirror Trophy, a four-boy team won Mr Crosfield's challenge shield for the 100 yards relay in competition against other local schools.

New Cricket Club - April 1906.

At the school sports of September 1912 the slow bicycle race was won by B. Wells in 75 seconds and the fast bicycle race by H.Shore in 153 seconds. If the course was the same the mind boggles, if longer then all is well. This same month the boys won the inter-schools swimming shield for the second consecutive year. The Boys' School was to win again in 1912, 1913 and 1914, come second in 1915 and win it twice more in 1916 and 1917.

New School at Earlswood

During these years there had been a considerable number of refusals of admission following the bans on new admissions to St John's Schools but there had also had been some movement of children in and out of the Schools and numbers had been reduced. On 31st August 1908 a new school at Earlswood opened and 48 infants moved there leaving only 93 infants on roll from a one time high of over 240. The Boys' School number was reduced to 254. A number of girls left reducing that department's number to 220.

The new schools, were built on the corner of St John's and Hooley Road on land previously belonging to the Royal Earlswood Asylum and containing the remains of the old gas works for that institution. The school was as modern as St John's was ancient, having central heating, being lit by electricity and having spacious halls and large windows that opened to provide adequate ventilation. Many parents were pleased to send their children there. Those from Earlswood benefited from a shorter journey, and parental concerns about the rise of motor traffic on the main road were no longer relevant. The builder was a local man, Mr E.Worsell of Redhill, who had his house in Grovehill Road backing onto his yard in Oakdene Road.

A New Classroom for the Boys' School

Proposals for an extension to the St John's Boys' School came to fruition on 2nd November 1908 when work started on building a new classroom at the south-east corner. Start of school was delayed until January 1909 when it was found that with only one fire in the room it was

A new classroom was added onto the south-east end of the Boys' School in 1908. The larger part of the building, the classroom, and the smaller part, a cloakroom, seem to have been built at the same time.

very cold, although this was in keeping with the rest of the Boys' School. In 1910 temperatures in the winter were 40°F at start of school rising to 50°F at midday, and similar in 1911.

In April 1909 a second partition was provided in the main room. The first one was moved to a new position enabling the hall to now be divided into three almost equal sections. The following information is from the Boys' School logbook of the time.

Classrooms	Size	Boys actual no.	Boys approved no.
New east classroom	24' x 22'	53	50
North division of main room	25' x 22¾'	57	53
Mid division of main room	25' x 20¼'	50	45
South division of main room	25' x 20¼'	50	48
Old south east classroom	19½' x 18'	36	36
Old south west classroom	19½' x 18'	36	36
Actual accommodation		282	
Approved accommodation			268

Incidentally, it seems that the approach to the Girls' and Infants' Schools from the St John's Church side of the schools was originally via the path from the gate directly in front of the entrance to the lower building, the slope not being in existence then. As this entranceway was dug over in preparation for the new classroom pupils had to use the entrance gate from the common on the other side of the School.

Some of the old buildings as they were prior to 1910
This photograph, taken from the churchyard, shows St John's School after 1884, with the Boys'
School built in front of the original 1845 building. Immediately behind the original building is the
1861 clock tower and the rest of the 1860s additions, including the houses built on the site. In
Memories of Yesterday, *by Alan Ingram and Malcolm Pendrill, is a picture of the new tower being*
built, and part of the caption says that near the base of the old tower was a tablet to William Price
of Woodhatch, friend of St John's, who died in 1858, and that a schoolroom and the Master's
house were built by his widow in 1861 in his memory.

Rules and Regulations

In September 1908 evening continuation classes were started in the Boys' School. How successful they were is uncertain for they were aimed at boys who had left school and wanted to continue their studies. Many did not finish work until six o'clock and barely had time to walk a mile or so home, get their tea and then walk half a mile or more to the school in time for a 7 pm start. They were the lucky ones for many others worked until 7 pm and others until 8 pm. Some of these would have been shop assistants for whom hours were long and leisure time short. Evening school is also mentioned in the Girls' School logs, although no details are given.

In May 1909 a Borough Education Committee circular stated that as from the following January more time was to be allocated to the teaching of reading, writing and arithmetic. This was achieved by the reduction of the marching and other drills that the boys performed, and by a general cut in the time allotted to the teaching of other subjects.

On 24th June 1909 the rule was made no longer to admit children under five years of age, although any under fives at the school at that time were not excluded. In July 1910 this was amended by the Borough Education Committee so that children of four years of age could be admitted at the beginning of the term at which they became five.

A New School at St John's

In 1909 a log entry for the Infants' School 4th January reads, *'This school is now a 'Council' School.'* No explanation of the entry is given but it could be to do with the fact that the old upper buildings were soon to be demolished and a new school built for girls and infants. If in the future the Borough Council were going to be providing the funds and the financial maintenance of the upper building, assuming control from the church, then the change of name and status were necessary to reflect this. The Boys' School remained within church control and was unaffected.

During the 1909 summer holidays one of the Girls' School classrooms was demolished. No explanation for this advance work is given but it was presumably in preparation for the total demolition of the buildings to come. Hopefully it was necessary because it obviously made a bad accommodation situation even worse, prompting the Mistress to enter the enforced new accommodation arrangements in the logbook.

	Size of Present Rooms	Number in Room
Cloakroom	19' 8" x 12' 6"	
Schoolroom	18' x 45'	84
Large Classroom	16' 62" x 37' 3"	78
Small Classroom	14' 10" x 16' 6"	39

St John's School viewed before 1895.

THE NEW ST. JOHNS SCHOOLS.

PALATIAL NEW BUILDINGS OPENED AT REDHILL.

The new schools for the girls and infants at St. John's, Redhill, were open for inspection on Saturday afternoon and evening. Invitations were issued by Alderman F. E. Barnes, J.P. (Chairman of the Reigate Education Committee), and Mrs. Barnes, to the principal residents in the Borough, and among those present were: The Mayor (Alderman T. Gregory), Mr. and Mrs. F. E. Lemon, the Rev. and Mrs. A. Simmonds, Alderman G. Gilbert, J.P., Mr. O. C. Apted and Mrs. Apted, Mr. and Mrs. W. E. Bartlett, Mr. Mark Dean, Mr. G. W. Rundall, Mr. J. B. Crosfield, Mr. A. J. Learner, Mr. Alfred Smith (Town Clerk),

poses as smoke flue, ventilating shaft, clock tower, etc. The girls' school has a central hall and six classrooms, one for 60 scholars, one for 40, and four for 50 each. The infants' school has a small central hall and four classrooms. Cloakrooms with teachers' rooms over are placed near each entrance, and a basement provides for furnace, fuel, and storage. Latrines on the most approved arrangement stand detached. The buildings are lighted by electricity and heated by low pressure hot water.

The walls are brick, principally local, with stone dressings. In some places concrete construction has been adopted.

Photo]   FRONT VIEW OF THE NEW SCHOOLS.   [T. Ware.

Mr. A. Lund Newell (secretary to the Education Committee), Mr. C. J. Wilkinson, Mr. J. Jinks, and other ladies and gentlemen; with Mr. T. R. Hooper, the architect of the schools.

The visitors took full advantage of the opportunities provided for viewing the premises, and the greatest admiration was expressed on all sides at the thoroughly up-to-date planning and equipment of the schools.

The new buildings which occupy the site of the former parochial schools are pleasantly situated on the southern slope of the hill, commanding an extensive view over the Weald. They form a somewhat picturesque group with their windowed gables, tiled roofs, and tower, a feature which answers such various pur-

Most of the floors have been laid by specialists. The plan and general design and details are in conformity with the regulations of the most approved modern elementary school buildings.

The heating was carried out by Haden and Sons, the lighting by T. S. Marriage and Co., the repairs and re-erection of the clock (from old school) by A. Cooling, of Redhill. Crosby and Co. were the builders, and T. R. and V. Hooper the architects.

Afternoon tea was provided, Messrs. Whitmore and Co. being the caterers.

Later in the day the schools were thrown open for inspection by the public, and were visited by large numbers of parents and friends of the scholars, for whose benefit they have been erected.

The article from the Surrey Mirror announcing the new St John's Schools and its 'Palatial New Buildings' Courtesy Surrey Mirror

The School on the Common

Views from the top of Redhill Common. This picture was taken before 1910 and shows the old school buildings, with the Master's and Mistress's houses on their right. On the far right of picture is the end of the row of Carters Cottages.

DANNS SERIES

VIEW FROM REDHILL COMMON

Redhill, View from Common.

After 1910 the new tower raises itself above the trees. Note how clear the common was, today it's a lot more overgrown and it can easily be seen how ideal the path once was for tobogganing in the winter. The depressions on the upper part of the slope are possibly the sites of early gravel diggings.

Apart from driving the fan, electricity also lit the upper building. A look around it today, however, reveals a number of gas points at various locations for lighting and heating, so a belt and braces approach had been adopted. The lower building was still lit solely by gas and would continue to be so until electric lighting was installed in 1921.

The situation was very similar to that of the Boys' School before the screens were erected, with several classes in the schoolroom together and a number of teachers talking at the same time.

In 1910 the teachers were able to take time off to visit the new school at Earlswood, an exciting time for them for they were to get a school much the same very shortly. It would seem that the new Girls' School was already being built, for St Johns Infants' Schools closed on 18th March 1910 for two weeks while the remainder of the old buildings were demolished, and recommenced two weeks later in two classrooms of the new Girls' School. In the May Mr Jinks took the opportunity to suggest to the Borough Education Committee that there was now plenty of cheap stone rubble on site with which to make up the boys' playground, for some time in a very poor state. Whether his suggestion was acted upon is unknown. If it was perhaps much of the old school is still on site.

The present tower, showing ventilation inlets alongside the clock.

After the summer holidays, on 29th August, the Infants' School was able to take over its own part of the building, although only three classrooms and a cloakroom were ready. This was not a calamity as after transference of children to the upper school there were only 87 infants on roll. Eventually four 23' x 19' classrooms and a 35' x 20' hall were available for 200 children.

Here then was the culmination of a great deal of work by the new Borough Education Committee and years of waiting by local schools. New facilities at Frenches Road, Earlswood and St John's had been built, and the old St John's buildings dating from a very long Victorian age had been swept away. Today we have left just a few photographs and plans of these old buildings and, perhaps feeling a little nostalgic, might wish we could travel back in time to see what they were really like. Were we to do so probably most of that nostalgia would vanish and we would be thankful that our recent generations of children have had the advantages of heat, light and ventilation that their predecessors did not. We cannot say that the upper building is perfectly attuned to the 21st Century, for as this history is written there is only four years to its centenary, but the very fact that we continue to use it says a great deal for its construction and design.

The Boys' School is 26 years older. It had needed two partitions so the main room, or hall, could be divided. Presumably partitions in the new upper building were a part of the original specification, as no mention of their later provision is made in subsequent log books. Many local dignitaries were present at the official opening of the new school in October 1910. The architects were the Redhill firm of Messrs T R and V Hooper. The old clock was re-installed in the new tower.

Also it ought to be said that the Borough Education Committee had not been formed at a time when all was well with local schools. It had inherited a poor situation, one of a history of under-funding and over-crowding, so if the years 1903-1908 had been lean ones then the benefits were realised in 1908-1910.

1910 - 1913

The Boys' School was used as a polling station in the parliamentary election of January 1910. This shut the Boys' School and reduced attendance at the Boys' and Infants' Schools as parents felt that the number of cars coming to St John's put their children in danger.

The School on the Common

Following the death of King Edward VII the children of were marched on 11th May 1910 to the Market Hall to hear the proclamation of King George V. The grandest occasion of the year was the late King's funeral but there was another notable funeral that year, that of Florence Nightingale. The events that made her famous took place in the Crimean War of 1854-56, and this might be an appropriate point to remind ourselves that St John's School was already ten years old at that time. Two famous writers also died in 1910, Leo Tolstoy and Mark Twain.

In June a number of boys were late to school and gave as their reason that they were helping get furniture out of houses threatened by a big fire at Earlswood.

An entry in the Girls' School log book is intriguing: - *'During the summer the two classes will spend the last hour on Friday afternoon 3.15 to 4.15 in the enclosed part of the common. The lessons taken will be stories ½ hour, games ½ hour.'* This may be a reference to the area where, as mentioned earlier in this chapter, a tennis court had been laid out on the common in July 1902 – surely it must have been enclosed and with a grass surface – or it may refer to one of two sites on the top common where clumps of trees were planted and ring-fenced in 1887 and 1897 as part of Queen Victoria's Jubilees.

In July a Boys' School parent was complaining that her son had got splinters from his desk seat. This was not the only case, for the offending furniture was 26 years old. The situation was remedied by the planing and varnishing of desks in the summer holidays. The school was proud of the fact that during the past four years fourteen boys had won scholarships to the Grammar School. Perhaps the ever-present possibility of splinters in the rear end from old desk seats had been their inspiration to work hard and get away from St John's.

Electricity had been supplied to the new building and drove the cooling fan that was situated in the tower alongside the clock. A log of 1911 tells us of its use: *'The large electric fan has been set in motion each day this week and has made a decided difference in the air of the rooms. Standard IV is immediately over the boiler and towards the end of the morning and afternoon sessions the air has been such as to cause extreme lassitude in both teacher and children, so much so that it was impossible to continue work. As a remedy the children had been sent to run round the playground and back while the room was thoroughly ventilated and refilled with fresh air. Now the fan performs the necessary change but must be used regularly to be of benefit.'*

When the fan in the upper building was taken out of use is unknown, as is where the control point for it was. It seems that the ventilation system might have worked by air being drawn into the roof and passing through ceiling vents into the two halls. Original classroom doors, since replaced and now stored in the roof area, had grills fitted for the air to pass into the classrooms and out through wall vents.

The social classes and school classes were connected by the domestic requirements of the former and the syllabus of the latter, as demonstrated by the following log entry detailing the Mistress' problems in catering for both: *The Head Mistress would like to give time to the elder girls who will leave shortly. The greater number become domestic servants and would therefore benefit by a home training course. This could be easily managed if the Head Teacher could plan a special time table and teach the smaller number, but the lower classes are too large to combine and there are only five assistants for seven standards.* The problem was discussed with the other staff members who agreed that it was too great to overcome, and the home training course was left out of the syllabus for this year.

By June 1911 the number of infants on roll had risen to 150, the number of senior girls to over 200, and both Head Mistresses wrote to the Borough Education Committee asking for another Assistant Mistress in each department. The reply was that a review of the staffing of all schools would take place in July and no extra staff would be forthcoming before the summer break. The considerable problems of staffing were not resolved until February and March 1912 when additional teachers were supplied by the Education Committee.

Mr Jinks and two unidentified Boys' School teachers with the 1911 football team

In 1911 woodwork classes at the Redhill Technical Institute were started for some of the boys, and Boys' pupil H.F. Welsh was mentioned in the Daily Mail for submitting an essay on standard bread in a national competition. On 22nd June a tea was given for the children to mark the Coronation of King George V, but it had to be given in the classrooms as it was a wet day. Two days holiday followed and hopefully they were sunny.

In the Boys' School during January 1912, teacher Mr Garton, already in the Head's bad books for dismissing boys when he had been told not to, was reported to the Managers and the Borough Education Committee for hitting a boy on the head with a ruler. On the 29th of that same month Mr Jinks was alerted by the crying of a boy in a classroom and found that he too had been hit on the head by Mr Garton, this time by chalk thrown at him. This was another question of how long the teacher would last – he was gone by 28th June.

Departures

A library was started in the Boy's School in October 1912. When the Boys' School moved to Sandcross Lane in 1954 the library was moved to an Earlswood school. Whether it had existed continuously between the two dates is unknown. In 1912 the departure of the library was something for the fairly distant future but the following year of 1913 was a year of departures. At the end of January the Rev. J.M.Gordon left the Parish after 30 years. He had taken over from the Rev. Henry Gosse as vicar of St John's Church and as Chairman of the Management Committee in 1892. In June the funeral took place of Mr Oram, who like the Rev. Gordon had been a member of the Management Committee for 30 years. An entirely different departure was made by a pupil who was expelled from the Boys' School for acting indecently in front of the girls.

Yet another departure, this time in 1913, was that of Her Majesty's Airship Delta. This airship had landed the day before in a field at Masons Bridge with a damaged rudder and had now been repaired. On 2nd July attendance in all school departments dropped considerably when children went to see it leave. Marking the Girls' School registers was delayed until 2.30 pm as a consequence and the children released at 4.30pm. Many local people went to see it rise and continue its interrupted journey, and views of the airship in the field were shown at the Pavilion cinema in Redhill a few days later. Postcards of the scene change hands today for many times more than they cost when produced soon after the event.

One of the postcards of 1912 showing HMA Delta *receiving repairs to her rudder with crowds of onlookers near Earlswood Common.*

Times Present, Times Past

The opening words of chapter one stated that history of St John's School began in the days of Reigate Manor, 23 years before the Borough Council was formed. This occurred after a long campaign by local people, resulting in the incorporation of the Borough of Reigate, the election of Councillors, Aldermen and a Mayor in 1863. Reigate and Redhill had ceased to be controlled by the Lord of the Manor and a few other powerful landowners and began to be administered by a Council comprised of elected, and therefore accountable, representatives of the people. September 1913 was the 50th jubilee of this incorporation of the Borough. Local children, including those from St John's, marched to Reigate Lodge where, among others places, it was celebrated, and each received a commemorative medal.

In 1909, when the new classroom had been built onto the Boys' School, Mr Jinks had started complaining about the temperatures in the classrooms. Five years later, in January 1914, new stoves were finally fitted and temperatures in all classes were recorded at 55–60°F. For once the classrooms in the Boy's School were warm in winter, but considering the building had been new in 1884, and if temperatures had been 50°F or lower in the classrooms during the coldest months since 1909, then they must have been like it every winter since the Boys' School was built.

Chapter Five
World War One

The Years of the First World War

The Mayor of Reigate was present at the prize-giving of 1912 and in his speech said that it was a pity that boys had to leave school at 14 for another two years could do so much for them. More significantly he went on to emphasise the value of military training and urged them to join the Territorials.

Such a statement reflected the tension of the times and indicates that conflict was a real possibility. By August of 1914 the possibility had become reality and school opening times were altered in December to reflect the circumstances of the darkened streets and billeting of troops in the Borough. All elementary schools were to open for afternoon sessions at 1.45 pm and close at 3.45 pm (infants) and 4 pm (senior). This was repeated in the winters of 1915-18 and was continued thereafter.

Day-to-day life became different in ways children might have found it difficult to understand. There were a great number of soldiers billeted in Redhill and many St John's children would have had one or more lodged in their house. Air raids and invasion were a threat, although in the event the former was not a problem locally and the latter did not happen. Neverthless many parents made their children fold their clothes neatly in bundles at night where they could quickly find them in the dark if the worst were to happen. In December, when the war was four months old, Mr Jinks was required to make a return concerning the names of children whose fathers were in the army or navy, and sent back 27 names in all.

The Boys' School had to be closed on 1st March 1915 as it had been occupied by soldiers over the previous two nights and had been left in a less that usable state. The floors were smeared with a mixture of dubbin, grease and jam and the caretaker was ordered to scrub them clean before the boys were allowed to return. In April, Hooley School was also unexpectedly closed, throwing a number of children onto the common to play. Whether this closure also had anything to do with the war only that school's logbooks would tell us, but some of the St John's boys were also absent, not having been able to resist the opportunity to join their friends.

On 1st May 1915 twenty children were admitted to the Infants' School from the Meadvale School. Seventeen more were admitted on 17th May and a log entry recorded, *'The Meadvale School is now closed...'* which referred to infants department only. With other admissions the numbers on role at the Infants' School had risen considerably to 204, although 73 went up to the senior departments that September. Numbers rose and fell but in June 1918 were back up to 204, with 55 children of class one being taught by the Head Mistress, 47 taught in class two by Miss Holroyd, 51 in class three by Mrs Newton, and the 51 children in classes four and five combined under Miss Whyman, a supply teacher with the same name as the Head. Whether the two were related is not known.

The Mayor, Mr Ince, had been present at the 1914 prize-giving and he returned on Empire Day 1915. Presumably the flag was raised on this occasion. He stressed the special significance of the Day because of the present state of conflict and took away with him a sum of money donated by the children to the Overseas Fund in aid of comforts for men serving abroad with the colours. Many funds for 'comforts' for men at the front existed. Examples of comforts were tobacco, briar pipes, cigarettes, ointment, foot powder, papers, postcards, socks - anything to make life at the front a little more comfortable. By the end of November 1914 the children had made donations totalling £5.5.0 and hoped to pay £1 a week towards the support of a little Belgian girl in the Presbyterian Church Home. In addition they had made 40 housewives (repair kits containing needles and cotton etc.) for soldiers off to the front and were attempting to make 50 pairs of socks and as many mittens as possible by Christmas. Whether or not this work was additional to or instead of some lessons is unknown.

On the 21st April 1915 there was a 'Patriotic Sale' at the Market Hall, Redhill - nothing to do with St John's - for the purpose of raising money for the benefit of soldiers at the front. The Market Hall buildings were also used as a clothing depot, some of the items purchased but by far the larger amount donated. The Mayoress of Reigate, Mrs Ince, was closely involved, for in January 1916 she had filled a quota of 100 mufflers and 100 pairs of mittens to be sent to France and was working on a further request for items to be sent to a military hospital by the end of the month. She launched an appeal for the materials, or for the money to buy them, and the women of the clothing committee held a meeting at which it was foreseen that such needs would be continuous to the war end, and a centre where people could make them was required. The provision of clothing and comforts for the sick and wounded, and for men at the front, was also in hand with sewing parties at Reigate Red Cross and at other organisations. This voluntary work, it was warned, should not be carried too far lest it deprive the poorer classes of earning a living.

The initials LEA, for Local Education Authority, appear in the Boys' School logs during January 1916 for the first time. Also for the first time certificates were awarded at prize giving instead of prizes as a wartime economy measure. Light woodworking classes had been started in the Boys' School to supplement classes at Redhill Technical College and some old desks in the basement of the Girls' School were used to make woodwork benches. Woodwork tools were ordered from Messrs Gillham, which was the forerunner of the present Mortons the Padlock hardware store at the top of Brighton Road, Redhill.

Boys were admitted from the Meadvale School in April 1916 when their department also closed (infants closed previous year). No record of the Girls' School department of the Meadvale School closing, assuming there was one, is contained in the St John's Girls' School logs.

The First World War, at its beginning, was thought not to be a war that would last too long. It was known by various names as it progressed. 'The War That Would Be Over Within A Year' was how it was viewed by many young men who readily volunteered for service early on in order to go to the front and 'teach the Hun a thing or two'. The fact that the reality was a horrific existence in appalling conditions rapidly changed that conception, and names such as 'A Fight to the Finish' and 'The War to End All Wars' were substituted. The loss of life was so great that by 1916 there were far fewer volunteers and conscription was initiated in the May. Two St John's teachers, Mr Young and Mr Kettle, went to Guildford for medical inspections on May 17th. Mr Kettle was declared exempt but Mr Young was declared fit and left for military service on May 29th, a traumatic time for both him and his wife, who was also a teacher at St John's.

The last third of the year saw the swimming trophy won again, the early closing of the school for the winter repeated, and a book belonging to the school burnt in one of the stoves because it had been in use by a boy with scarlet fever.

The 1917 prize giving had certificates instead of prizes again, and on Empire Day the Mayor presented a picture to the school. The swimming shield was won for the sixth time in seven years and Mrs Young was granted leave to be with her husband, who was home on leave from France.

A problem with the Boy Scouts cropped up. This was because the funeral of a figure in the movement had 21 St John's boys applying for leave to attend. The LEA (there's those initials again) decreed that four could go and the rest had to remain at school. A ballot was held and the four were chosen. Then all 21 went to the funeral. An apology was afterwards received from Scout Leader Mr Makovski but came in a letter from no less a person than Sir Jeremiah Colman of Gatton, something difficult not to accept with some grace.

Food queues were commonplace in 1918. The writer of this history had the good fortune to interview a Mrs Martin in the early 1990s, a lady who remembered WW1 quite well. About food she had several things to say, part of which was, *"As the war went on food got tighter and tighter. We didn't seem to be short of clothes, just food. I heard talk of merchant ships being sunk, and we got less and less. Children would queue for food as soon as we heard there was some somewhere. There was a place that sold potatoes, Reddy's I believe it was, and when you heard they had some in you headed there. You queued, and as soon as it got to your turn that's when there was none left. Another place we used to go was a shop called the Maypole in the High Street. It sold only margarine. Directly one person said there was something to eat in a shop you queued for it. Food wasn't rationed to my knowledge, not in the First War."*

Her references are to shops in Redhill, and her words are reflected in the logs of the Boys' School for 1918:-

January 22nd	*40 boys absent on food queues*
January 24th	*36 boys absent on food queues*
January 29th	*50 boys absent on food queues*
February 5th	*35 boys absent on food queues*
February 12th	*30 boys absent on food queues*

A sign of how hard life was getting is given in the additional entry:-

February 6th   *Communal food kitchen opened today.*

Another indication of the times appears in a return made by Mr Jinks about the health of the boys at St John's:-

Partially blind	2
Partially deaf	1
Epileptic	1
Pulmonary Tuberculosis	3

After all this it comes as no surprise that on March 8th the school's turret clock *'kept bad time this week and stopped altogether on Friday'.* Time itself, by the way, had been altered in May 1916 when the Summer Time Bill came into force. All clocks were advanced one hour, which meant it was darker in the mornings but lighter in the evenings. The purpose was to reduce the hours during which artificial lighting was required and thereby save a great amount of coal needed for the war effort.

The absence of many fathers and older brothers fighting abroad meant that families lived on money sent home plus government allowances paid according to the number of school-age children in the family. Worst of all was the loss of those fathers and brothers. Mothers lost sons, wives lost husbands and children lost fathers. Many young women lost fiancées, some unable to overcome the heartbreak and remaining spinsters all their lives as a result. Little is known about ex-St John's boys in WW1, but one, Arthur George Knight, son of Mrs E.H.Knight of Somerset Road, was posthumously awarded the VC for leading a charge in which he killed a German officer and two NCOs and captured twenty men. How tragic that after such heroism he should have been killed by a shell while returning to his unit shortly afterwards. A victim of the slump in the building trade he had gone to Canada in 1910, joining an Alberta regiment and spending three years in France.

On Empire Day 1918 Mr Hull again made an address; no doubt it was full of patriotism. Mr Hull had been at the forefront in urging the young men of the Borough to join the colours and had chaired meetings to determine how those who had not done so could be persuaded. It must be remembered that we who look back may not consider the danger of invasion as real in WW1 as it was in WW2, but to the older folks of the day, those who knew they would not themselves be going to the front, they had only the younger generation to rely upon for protection.

The Mayor was again present at the school on this occasion and the logbook records that he, *'presented a picture of the Queen.'* Although King George V was on the throne at the time, and there is an anonymously pencilled question mark against the word 'Queen', the reference would seem to be to his wife, Queen Mary.

Conscription continued, with Boys' Schoolteachers Mr Bath being classed grade two at his July medical, and Mr Woodroofe noted as away on military service in September. Mr Woodroofe was born in 1863 and was aged 55 at the time, so perhaps his service was with the Volunteer Force, the equivalent of the Home Guard in WW2. He and a colleague at the Boys' School, Mr Kettle, who was 41, were two teachers who were older than those normally employed at St John's. A list of the 19 other teachers appointed since 1900 shows an average age of 24-25, and the first thought occurring to the compiler of this history was that they might not have been employed at St John's if it had not been for the war and the absence of younger men. This thought would, however, have been at least in part an error, for Mr Woodroofe was appointed in October of 1913, before the war started. Mr Kettle's appointment date was December 1914.

From 22nd October to 4th November 1918 all the schools in the Borough were closed because of an outbreak of influenza. One week later, on the 11th of November, before 11 am, there were rumours circulating that an armistice had been signed. The date of WW1 on the war memorial at Shaws Corner, Redhill, is 1914-19. This is because the armistice was a temporary cessation of hostilities that was finally ratified in the summer of the year after the guns ceased firing. Then, at 11.15, the news was received. The war that would always be known as the 'Great War' was over. At 11.40 am the Rev. B.Slater, Vicar and Chairman of the Managers, came to the school with the confirmation that Armistice had indeed been signed. A short service of thanksgiving was arranged and followed by three cheers for the good news. The children were told there would be a half-holiday and dismissed. Much would not revert to normal for some time but at least the guns were silent.

Those Who Were There

Arthur Terry

Arthur was at St John's during WW1 and remembers the Boys' School head Mr Jinks. According to Arthur the troops were good friends to the school as they used to secretly dump tins of corned beef in the school bins for the poorer children to take home. He said that on the common nearby was a remount, a place where horses were kept until needed to replace those killed in France. He remembers the laundry next to the school, the Fountain pub (now gone) as well as the Elm Shades, 'Gears' the undertakers, and 'Gerry Hawkins' the small shop where a farthing would buy an everlasting strip of liquorice or a sherbet dab.

Jack Moore

Another pupil, Jack Moore, remembers that food was indeed scarce. He became quite sick of the pea soup that was frequently on the menu at home. He had been fairly carefree, roaming the local woods and fields around Meadvale, until a lady had come to his house (possibly a School Manager) and suggested he attend school. He went to the Meadvale St John's Infants' School with Teachers Miss Robinson and Miss Peat but says that it was at St John's Boy's School where he learned to read and write and do simple sums (these teachers are pictured in chapter 7).

Conflict with other local boys was something frequently on his agenda, as was cheeking adults, so fight and flight were things he was familiar with. To his horror his mother had dressed him in a sailor suit when he was at Meadvale School. Where she had got it from he had no idea, as they were so poor that following the day his mother threw their only cups at his father, they had drunk from jam jars for months. The problem with the sailor suit was that it had the flap at the back, ideal for an adversary, boy or adult, to catch hold of in order to apprehend him. He remembers Miss Peat chasing him down Hardwick Road one day and catching him by getting hold of the flap. Limited freedom through sailor suit and school perhaps were factors that contributed to his memory of 1914, when he was at St John's, being a very long year.

A number of Belgian refugee children were admitted to St John's, the first one mentioned in the log books going by the splendid name of Cassiers Lion. On 31st December 1914, a Saturday, children gave entertainment in the central hall of the Girls' School in aid of the Belgian Refugees Fund. Threepence a head was charged for admission and £3.18.0 was raised. A number of Belgian children lived in Meadvale and Jack Moore remembers battles between them and local boys. The latter's ploy would be to taunt the Belgians and lure them down the hill from the copse and then, with reinforcements, chase them back up. The slope would slow their flight and make them easy to catch or bring them within range of stones hurled by the pursuers, or even better from the attackers point of view, air guns. This is not an example of the friendship and harmony the Belgian refugees found in other aspects of local life but is a good example of natural conflicts among children arising from perceived differences, whatever they might be.

Inevitably not all the refugees returned home after the war. One married a local girl and set up in business locally. He was still running Brems' radio and television shop in Clarendon Road in the 1940s.

Richard Farmer

Richard started aged five at St John's in 1915. When he went to the Boys' School Mr Jinks was still the Headmaster and is remembered as a short, bald, red-faced man. Mr Jinks retired in 1919 and was followed by Mr Oliver Gregson. Other teachers at the time were Mr and Mrs Young, Mr George (Fiddlesticks) Barnett, Tommy Bath (killed in his Earlsbrook Road home by a bomb during WW2), Mr (Splinters) Woodruff and caretaker Mr (Whacker) Ware.

Other boys Richard Farmer remembers at St John's at the time were George Wilshier, Albert Wickens, Arthur Shove, Charlie Pearce, and Arthur and Sydney Moore, the latter pair younger brothers of Jack Moore.

In summer 1919 a 'Comrades in Arms' Sports was held in Redhill. Richard Farmer has a cup presented to school children commemorating the end of WW1 that was presented at the sports ground but whether it was at these sports or a different occasion he does not remember. The following year inter-School Sports were held in the town, an event that became an annual one.

Post WW1

Normal service was resumed in the best possible way with the return to civilian life of Mr Young from military service in Germany - a life spared when so many were sacrificed. He went back to married life and teaching at St John's where the gas lighting had deteriorated to the point where reading by it was impossible. It was corrected by the replacement of piping and mantles so that the correct level of illumination within the school was restored.

But there was much change. Mr Jinks' retirement had been due in 1916 when he had completed 40 years service but he had stayed on because of the unsettled wartime conditions. Now, with the restoration of peace the time had come to go. There were two ceremonies concerned with his retirement, the first of which was at a meeting of the Borough Education Committee at which Mr Lemon was in the chair and at which a letter was presented to the retiree.

Tributes were made to Mr Jinks at this meeting. Although saying he would not make a speech (he joked he was a conscientious objector to making speeches) he nevertheless thanked everyone and went on to say that his ambition from the first was to do all he could to deserve success. He had come to Redhill when the population was but 13,000 and when the Rev. Gosse was vicar, and when there were only three schools - St John's, St Matthews and the Wesleyan. Although conscious as he was of how far his ambitions had fallen short of what he wanted them to be he had met with some success and was thankful.

Naturally the second ceremony was at St John's School. Mr F.C.Claridge, who for 30 years had been a manager of the schools, hoped that they would long have the Headmaster among them as friend and neighbour. Mr Jinks was presented with a gold watch, Mrs Jinks with a bouquet.

Mr Jinks made a speech of thanks in which he outlined his long history at the school, detailing its growth - if only we had a copy. Whether he mentioned the number of boys that had passed

Education Offices
Municipal Buildings
Reigate
    15th April 1919.

Dear Mr Jinks,

    In the name of the Reigate Education Committee I
am writing to express the high admiration felt by
its members of the long and faithful service by
you as headmaster during the past 42½ years. St
John's School has been one of the largest and most
successful schools in the borough, and you have
good reason to be proud of the record of your
work, and of the success of so many of your
pupils. It has fallen to your lot to train many
scholars, even to children's children, and to
watch the progress of succeeding generations.
    The Education Committee fully appreciate the
commitment with which you continued at your post
during the war years, although the time for your
retirement had arrived. We desire to join with the
managers and teachers of the school, the parents
of the scholars and others in wishing you health
and strength for many years to come, with much
happiness and enjoyment for your retirement.

    Frank E. Lemon
    Chairman of the Reigate Education Committee

The letter of thanks to Mr Jinks from the Education Committee

through St John's during his time there we cannot say, but a newspaper article later estimated it to be 3,300. Handed to Mr Jinks by the Rev. Slater were the following items: -

    A microscope in a case
    A wooden box of mounted specimens
    Two volumes of 'Marvels of the Universe'
    One volume 'Birds of Britain'
    One wooden case of minerals
    One wooden case of biblical subjects (not in over-good order)

Is it possible these were from when the Rev. Gordon had started elementary science lessons at his house in 1885? The action of Mr Jinks was to hand them on for the continued use of the school, an action repeated by each Headmaster thereafter up to and including Mr Bennett in 1953 when they cease to be recorded. Where are they now, we may wonder.

Following Mr Jinks as Headmaster of the Boys' School was Mr John Lancaster, who took temporary charge from 29th April 1919 until 1st July of that year when a new man became the new permanent Head. The log entry recording this his arrival states, *'I took charge of this school' today and was introduced to the scholars and teachers by the vicar.'* Short and sweet and to the point maybe, but without a name. Fortunately someone has added in pencil, 'O Gregson' so we may know who he was. Our thanks to that anonymous annotator.

On 29th July there was a Peace Celebration at the Sports Ground and each child received a celebratory mug to record the event. Shortly after this the summer break was one week longer than usual - the King's wish in order to celebrate peace.

In October, in the Boys' School, Nelson's Day was mentioned for the first time and was marked by an address and patriotic songs, and school broke up for mid-term holiday, the first mention of this too. In December the new Head, Mr Gregson, was making his presence felt. A log entry reads, *'I have again to report the weak and appalling discipline of Mr Bath, I have had complaints from other members of staff that they cannot work.'* We have seen entries like this before, and they usually resulted in the departure of the teacher concerned. This occasion was no exception, although Mr Bath did last longer than most. In October 1922 another log entry reads, *' I spoke again to Mr Bath about discipline and took matters to managers.'* Mr Bath resigned on 16th April 1922.

On the first anniversary of the signing of the Armistice there was a short talk in the hall at 11.45am and a two minutes silence as commended by HM the King. In 1920 there was a short service at 10.45am and the two minutes silence was at 11am. This became an annual ceremony repeated until 1938. On some years children were also taken to the memorial at Shaws Corner where in 1926, Princess Helena Victoria also attended.

War savings certificates were issued to children in the Borough as part of the effort to raise money for the War Loan. Several children from all three departments of St John's went to the Town Hall in early July of 1919 to get their certificates stamped. A half-holiday was awarded on the 16th when the sum collected reached £1000.

Irene Bundell was at St John's 1914-1928 and is the left of the front centre pair of girls directly in front of the maypole. Looking at the front five pairs of girls and numbering them 1-10 from the left they are: - 1. Unknown 2. Marjorie Shoubridge 3. Madeleine Young (both her parents were St John's teachers at the time) 4. Unknown 5. Irene Bundell 6. Phillis Jarvis 7 and 8 unknown 9. Violet Budd 10. Vera Parker. The teacher at the maypole is Miss Weekes and the other teacher is Miss Broughton. If a child was from a better off family they had white socks but if not the less expensive black ones. Information and photo courtesy Mrs Smith, daughter of Irene Bundell

Health and Sport

Since 1909 a school nurse had been visiting the school regularly to measure and weigh children and to carry out medical inspections. This was in addition to the visits of the Medical Officer of Health. All of the familiar ailments continued to affect children and teachers alike, causing the usual variations in attendance. The most probable benefit of additional medical attention was the earlier recognition of symptoms and the sending home of affected children to reduce the risk of spreading infection. Nevertheless the school was closed for a month in January 1917 by an outbreak of mumps and for two and a half months (including summer break) in the same year by measles and german measles. Diphtheria was still prevalent, as proved by the fact that the headmistress, Miss Whyman, caught it and was absent for eighteen weeks.

The question arises as to what the teachers did when a school was closed like this. The answer is that they went to work at other local schools with staff shortages. A Miss Bennett came to work at St John's from Frenches Road School when it was similarly closed for one month in May 1917.

From about 1915 games and physical training began to receive more attention, with a physical training advisor, Miss Brown, visiting the school regularly. After her December 1919 visit she wrote, *'It is a joy to see these children. They are so happy and free and the work is as delightful as ever,'* an entry which makes the reader feel happy too.

Chapter Six
The Nineteen-twenties

The Roaring Twenties

The 1920s began fairly uneventfully. The usual problems of illness and shortage of teachers continued, the circuses still visited and the Sunday schools still had their outings but otherwise things were normal. In early 1920 the first issue of the Boys' School magazine was delayed but not mentioned again, so we cannot know if it eventually appeared that year. If it did it possibly lasted only a short time for, six years later, in January of 1926, appears an entry, *'Decided to start a school magazine.'* What was decided in 1920 was that a concert would be held. Although there is no log entry to record it we can assume that it proved very successful for in 1923 is an entry, *'Day School concert. 3rd annual.'*

In April 1930 there were only 48 boys in the Infants' School compared to 90 girls. In the summer of 1921 the current logbook, in use since 1890, became full and a new one was started. Before that book was filled the Second World War would commence.

In June 1920 Mr E C P Hull presented a challenge cup for Boys' School sports, won for the first time by A Risbridger, a name that crops up a number of times, identifying him as good at sports. He was unable to win the 1920 inter-school sports single-handed however, and St John's came runners-up to Cromwell Road.

On 31st August the boys from the Meadvale Home were allowed to return to the Boys' School, some after seven and a half months away, infectious disease presumably being the reason. On 27th September two boys named Winyard were admitted from Bletchingley, which seems a long way to come, especially with winter imminent. In October a return was sent to the Education Office about jerseys: -

Number of boys on books	238
Number wearing jerseys	140
Jerseys bought from school	38
Colour adopted	Grey
School badge	Specimen sent

Reg Harriden, whose reminiscences appear later in this history, confirms that grey jerseys were still a part of boy's and girl's uniforms in the 1930s.

In 1921 an Austrian boy staying in the district was admitted to the Boys' School, as were two small boys who had been detained in Sweden at the outbreak of the Great War. On 11th February Mr Jinks paid a visit to the Boys' School. He had been retired for almost two years – was he finding life strange without a school to run we wonder? No doubt he found the school very cold for a terse log of 10th April reports: *'Temperature 40° - no fires for past ten weeks due to coal strikes'.* It goes on to say that fortunately the weather had been of the early summer variety, but adds: *'Today it snowed.'*

Two events deemed worthy of a day off for teachers and children alike were the wedding of Princess Mary on 28th February 1922 and the wedding of the Duke of York on 26th April 1923. The Duke married Lady Elizabeth Bowes-Lyon and in spite of being named Albert was to become King George VI in 1937. A half-day was also given for the visit locally of the Prince of Wales in

November 1923 when he came to attend a ceremony at the Police Orphanage at Redhill. Another was given for the visit of Princess Helena Victoria when she came to the service at the Shaws Corner war memorial on 8th November 1926.

'School closed, required for St John's Church Garden Fete,' reads an entry of 28th June 1922. An advantage to the church of St John's Boy's School being under its control was that the premises were available for such an event. The advantage of a day off for the children this year was lost in 1923, however, when the school merely closed for the church fete an hour earlier in the afternoon.

Charles Pearce was a pupil at St John's and would have gone to the Empire celebrations on the common and been addressed with all the other children by the Mayor. What he could not have dreamed of

The Football Team of 1922
Back Row - L-R: Ernest Young, Frank Risbridger, Arthur Moore, Fred Elsey, Charles Hutton, Albert Wickens
Front Row: - Sidney Loader, Charles Pearce, John Fenn, Joe Pickard, Lewes Miles, Harold Hewitt.

then (or perhaps he did) was becoming Mayor of Reigate himself one day, something he achieved when he became the 50th Mayor in 1971-72. It is not known if this was a singular feat or if any other Mayor was also an old pupil of St John's.

Charles Pearce is pictured above and left school at 13 to work as a telegraph boy. He was a Borough Councillor and formed his own band, playing at local dances for many years. Bert Wickens played football for Redhill. Charles Hutton was a good swimmer and worked at the old Redhill baths. Sid Loader's father owned a café in the Brighton Road. Joe Pickard worked at the gas works. Harold Hewitt became the common keeper. Arthur Moore worked on the TV Times for a number of years

Children were allowed time off to go to the cinema to see educational films such as *'Nature's Wonderland'* and *'The Life of a Butterfly'* in 1923. They would have gone either to the Cinema Royal in Station Road or the Pavilion Cinema in the High Street. In either case the films they saw would have been silent, 'talkies' not coming to Redhill until 1929.

Sport

Annual school swimming galas were in their fourth or fifth year when the older girls won the shield as the best local team. They had also won the netball shield and the athletics shield and so held all three shields competed for by local schools. The boys' shield was also won by St John's after a lapse of five years. In July 1924 the boys emulated the girls' 1923 feat by winning all three shields available to them in inter-school competition, triumphing in football, athletics and swimming (although they had also won the swimming shield in 1923). They won the sports shield in 1925 with 26 points from a possible 36, a record. The girls again won the sports shield at the 1926 inter-school sports, a feat they repeated in 1927 and 1928. In the latter year they also won every one of their netball matches against other schools. In 1927 and 1928 the boys won the sports shield for the fourth and fifth successive years. In 1930 the boys won the sports shield once more, making six years out of seven that they had held it. The girls also continued their run of success when they again won the netball shield after winning every game they played in the 1929-1930 season.

School Life and Activities

Armistice Day 1923 was marked not only by two minutes silence but also by placing flowers at the foot of the church memorial that had been erected by the lychgate in 1920. It has no names on it but inside the church a roll of honour commemorates the 195 men and one woman of the Parish who went to war and did not return.

In 1918-1919 there had been a world wide flu epidemic and from time to

The 1923-24 St John's Athletics team
Back Row: - Shove, Peace, Merrick, Parker, Funnell, Cawtheray
Middle Row: - Terry, Sidney Moore, Bristow.
Front Row: - Elliott, Wade

time the school had closed because of various outbreaks of diseases. In 1924 so many staff were struck down by flu that the Headmistress was left as the only staff member in the infants' school.

On 29th February 1924 there was the first ever dental inspection of infants and upper girls. It did not take as long as it might have done a few years earlier as the number on role had dropped to 90, the lowest figure since 1910. By September 1926 the number was up to 188 and the Head Mistress was asking the Managers to recommend the Borough Education Committee to appoint another teacher, which they agreed to do.

The Misses Ramsay seem both to have been School Managers. Presumably they were sisters, although this is not certain. Other members of the Ramsay family had been associated with the school and although it is recorded in March 1924 that, 'Miss Ramsay, manager of the school for many years, buried today', a Miss Ethel Ramsay continued to fill a Manager's role into the 1940s. Other local ladies were prominent at the prize giving of that year, when Mrs Blakesly of Fairlawn gave the prizes with Mrs Makovski in the Chair. In June Mr Claridge, who had been associated with the school for forty years, resigned. The end of 1924 saw the departure of (the almost anonymous) Mr O.Gregson and the arrival of new Boys' School Head Mr H.C.Cole.

1925 saw the death of the Queen Mother, Alexandra, consort of King Edward VII. A hymn was sung in school in her memory. The vicar, the Rev. Erskine Clarke, presented the 1925 school prizes but died in the March of 1926 and was succeeded

The 1923-24 St John's Football Team
Back Row: - Young, Cawtheray, Humphrey, Hoar, Humphrey
Front Row: - Parmentor, Hindard, Lane, Wright, Terry, Pickard

The School on the Common

by the Rev. L.G. Mannering.

In September the Boys' School annual outing was revived. Forty-seven boys visited various London places of interest and finished at the Cenotaph where they, *'laid a wreath in the memory of old scholars who died in the Great War; a moving ceremony'.* An enquiry was made about war orphans by a Miss Ballantine who called at the school from the Pensions Office in February 1926. The reality was that another war was only fourteen years away and children at St John's were now old enough to be eligible to fight in it.

Cobham's seaplane is watched by admirers on Westminster Bridge as it touched down on the Thames at the end of an historic 1926 return flight to Australia. This was at a time when engines were in use in sufficient numbers for horses to have become used to the sound of them. See next page.

Also in 1926 the Common Conservators gave permission for St John's children to use the 'Lawns' for organised games as long as they were supervised and wore suitable shoes so the turf was not damaged. The Common Conservation body is long gone and there is now no management of the non-golfing part of the common as there once was.

A radio was purchased for the Girls' School in 1926 from the proceeds of a jumble sale and nature study lectures were listened to on it. Also listened to was Cobham's return in October 1926 from his great pioneering flight of 28,000 miles to Australia and back. Alan Cobham had entered the Royal Flying Corps in 1917. In 1921 he joined Geoffrey de Havilland's new aircraft company, for which he undertook a succession of long-distance flights: 5,000 miles around Europe; 8,000 miles across Europe and North Africa; 12,000 miles through Europe to Palestine, Egypt, along the North African coast, and back through Spain; plus return flights to the Cape of Good Hope. It was the return from his famous, and the first ever flight to Australia and back, which the St John's girls listened in to, and after which he was knighted.

The radio was also used for history, English and music broadcasts. These were the early days of broadcasting, when BBC stood for British Broadcasting Company, becoming a Corporation the following year under direction of John Reith, and radios in schools must have been enough of an innovation then for an engineer from the BBC to call to advise on their use.

On 27th February 1927 Mr Jinks died. Considering the length of his service at the School - his entries in the Boys' School logs span the years 1876 to 1919 - one might have expected to see more than the fact of his death followed simply by, '*His life and work at the school were mentioned at dismissal*', although perhaps he would have been satisfied with that. Equally economical is the tone of the log dealing with the funeral; '*Funeral of above. Representative members of the boys, Headmaster and three assistants attended by permission of LEA. Timetable adjusted so work delayed as little as possible.*' Quite possibly he would have approved of that too. His grave is on the right at the very top of the steps leading from Pendleton Road to St John's Church, a position of honour, it seems, for a man whose forty-two and a half years at St John's School is unlikely to be exceeded.

1926 was the year of the General Strike, from May 4th-12th. Teachers from the Infants' School and Girls' School remained at work and received a letter from the Borough Education Committee regarding their loyal service. Swimming lessons had to be stopped during the miners' strike later that summer due to lack of coal for use in the boilers. Needless to say, these were difficult years for many workers in Britain. The Welsh miners, who were forced back to work, suffered accordingly. At the end of 1928 St John's children sent a box of food and clothing to the South Wales mining district and gave a concert at which two guineas was sent to the Mayor's Fund for the Relief of Miners.

In January 1929 the secretary of the Borough Education Committee visited '*to see the effect of the new electric lamps which still give insufficient light on dark afternoons*'. The new electric lights were installed in 1921 and it would be wonderful to know how much better they were than the gas lighting that had until then illuminated the buildings, and whether the gas lighting had completely fallen into disuse at the same time. Hopefully it gave immediate improvement but no doubt incurred quite an expense; part of the proceeds from that year's concert going to the Installation of Electric Lighting Fund. Better or not, the level of light provided was still insufficient for the outcome of the Borough Education Secretary's visit. The recommendation was that 60 candle-power bulbs be replaced by 100 candle-power bulbs (probably quite dim compared to modern 60 and 100 watt light-bulbs). Some of the old gas connections still exist in parts of school and the gas fire in the old staff room, now the Headteacher's office, although non-functional for many years, was removed in May 2000.

1920s Awards

On 24th June 1924 a boy at the Infants' School named Percy Pattenden fell in the playground and cut his chin badly. He was sent home in charge of his sister, which must have been a rare absence for him for he was later to get an award for high attendance during his time at St John's. Lillian Jobson received a special certificate on 31st March 1926 for six years perfect attendance. It was presented on behalf of the Borough Education Committee by its Chairman, Councillor Temple Newell, and she also received a silver watch engraved with the name of the school and the date 1921-1926 by Alderman H.Crosfield. If hers was a record it was broken in 1937 by Sylvia Beadle who completed seven years perfect attendance. She too was presented with a certificate and a watch by the Managers. (Since writing this an eight year perfect attendance certificate, 1917-1924, belonging to Richard Farmer has come to light)

From Pupil to Teacher

Mildred Chillingworth was a pupil of the Girls' School from 1921-1927 and remembers using slates as an infant and pen and ink as a junior. She also remembers having a doll's house to play with and the girls sketching each other in drawing classes. Exercise lessons were a mixture of stretching and agility exercises coupled with marching drills similar to the boys. There was also rounders on the common. She won a scholarship to the County School and became a teacher, she returned to St John's School in this capacity from 1937-1947. There is more about Mildred later in this history when, as Mrs Barratt, she returned to St John's.

Reminiscences of the 1920s

Millicent Barnard

Millicent started in the Infants' School in 1922 or 1923 and remembers Miss Whyman as *'an old lady'*. Millicent's mother had taught her and her sisters how to sew and knit and she had to show one of the boys in her class how to knit. She also remembers Miss Towell in the Girls' School -*'a very stern lady and we were all afraid of her'* she kept a cane behind a picture by her desk in the main hall. There were also teachers Miss Lees, Miss Hartnell, Miss Griffin, and Miss Blyth.

Millicent played in the netball team and treasured the medal she won. Sadly it was stolen from her in a burglary. She loved the nature walks over the hills and, as she lived close to the school, spent most of her youth on Earlswood Common. She remembers, too, the Empire Day celebrations on Mill Street 'Flats', the point on the common described earlier. The girls wore their best white dresses and a daisy.

Millicent also remembers a glass cabinet in the Girls' School hall that was full of all sorts of old things. The children were never allowed to open it to have a proper look. A *'very nice lady'* came once a week to take gym, and the nit nurse came once a month - *'we all hated that'* - but overall she remembers her days in the Infants' and Girls' Schools as happy ones.

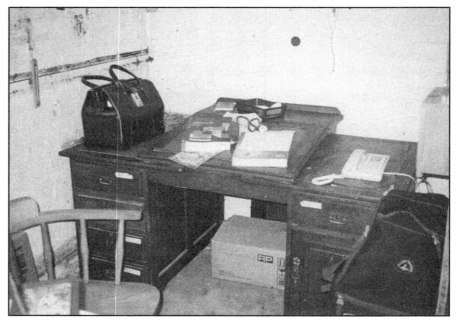

This desk has been stored in the basement for many years and could well be the one used by a succession of Heads, including Miss Whyman, in the main hall.

Phyllis Cooper

Phyllis lived at 1 Carters Cottages and was at St John's during 1921-1930. She confirms that Miss White was very strict and remembers that she and Miss Griffith lived together. Phyllis and friends would sometimes act as ball girls after school for Miss White, Miss Griffith and other teachers when they played tennis on the court set up in the playground. She also remembers the very large boot scraper by the entrance doors, her memory of it being painfully clear, as she fell over it one day and scraped her leg instead of her shoe. One of the jobs the girls sometimes had was to fill the inkwells with ink made up from powder.

Across Pendleton Road were some shops: Terry's general store (probably the Gerry Hawkin's shop of Arthur Terry's day), Hall's shoe repairs, Mr Gear's undertakers and Sid Ware's greengrocery - Phyllis remembers his horse was stolen from a shed on the common where it was kept. The Fountain pub was still there and run by Mr and Mrs Whyman. She says that sometimes the pub's piano would be hauled across the road onto the small piece of green below the church between Fountain and Pendleton Roads and parties held there in good weather. When the laundry chimney was being repaired Phyllis used to get into trouble for climbing the ladder when the workmen were not there.

Phyllis was also able to confirm that there was a distinction between the 'Flats' and the 'Lawns', the former being that part of the common by Mill Street, where the Empire Day celebrations were always held, the latter being the higher, level areas between Mill Street and the Top Common where the school sports were often held. An aspect of the common land opposite the Plough that Phyllis also remembers was Payne's pond - ducks and tadpoles - which no longer exists.

Phyllis went to work in the laundry next to the school and is the mother of John Clarke, the caretaker of St John's who retired in September 2000. The caretaker in Phyllis' day was Mr Ware.

Boy Scouts

Mr H.C.Cole, the then Headmaster of the Boys' School, was approached by one of his pupils in 1928 with the suggestion that the school have a scout troop. A number of boys had been away to camp at Rustington with him and had enjoyed the experience, hence the suggestion. Nothing was done at that time but even more boys went to the Isle of Wight camp the following year and the request was made again. A scout group, the 16th Reigate, had existed at Meadvale since 1913 but a separate group, the 34th Reigate was formed at St John's school in 1930.

The End of the 1920s

The 1920s probably rank as the worst for sick absence among the Infants' School teachers, many of them having illnesses such as pleurisy more than once and being off school for considerable periods and requiring numerous supply teachers to cover. Miss M.Whyman resigned from the Infants' School with effect from 31st May 1929 after three months' serious illness with bronchitis and pleurisy, not a good way to end either the decade or her 24 years at St John's.

In this picture, taken in 1927-8 at Redhill Sports Ground during St John's School sports day, Lorna Dyer is on the left. With her are Thomas Jarman and Daisy Girding. No longer living in the Redhill area, Lorna missed the history evening held at the School in July 2000 but following a telephone call she was put in touch with ex-classmate Freda Bundell and they were able to plan a reunion after not seeing each other since their school days. Picture courtesy Lorna Fredersdorff, née Dyer.

The School on the Common

According to the logs the decade was also a very bad one for the children, with a number of entries referring to 'epidemics'. Certainly more was being written about poor attendance through illness and it may have been that Miss Whyman's style of log writing for the Infants' School tended to emphasise that part of school life more than others had done. The logs of the Girls' School also record much illness, however, and there is no denying the seriousness of the illnesses, including diphtheria, that were constantly affecting and infecting the children. Worst of all was the death of infant Gladys Terry in October 1929, *'a little pupil'* for whom the rest of the children brought pennies to the value of 15/- for flowers in her memory plus a donation to the East Surrey Hospital where she died. For her the 'roar' of the twenties was silenced forever. Incidentally 1928 was the year of the discovery of penicillin by Alexander Fleming.

This is not to paint the 1920s over entirely with shades of doom and gloom because many good things were happening. Children were taken on school trips more; there had been trips to a London museum and zoo, and to the Tattoo at Aldershot amongst others, and locally to the Redhill Gas Works and elsewhere. There were nature and picnic excursions on Redhill Common and Reigate Downs, all in the tradition apparently begun by Miss Greening in 1902. Children competed against other schools in athletics, netball, football and swimming, went to the baths at Reigate and benefited from facilities at Earlswood School. They listened to radio broadcasts and had lectures given by people who came to the school to talk about their experiences abroad. They were mixing more, getting more worldly experience and tasting the success of competition possibly more than at any other time in the school's history.

Children of the 1920s
The left hand picture shows children, local to St John's, standing close to the School with Carters Cottage's and Kings Avenue in the background. The little girl second from right in the back row is Alice Atkins.
The right hand picture was taken in September 1924 and Alice Atkins is the girl on the left. Some, if not all of these children, would have gone to St John's School. Alice Atkins became a helper there. These two pictures were kindly given by Mary Peters, who appears in one of the 1930s classroom pictures.

Chapter Seven
The Nineteen-thirties

Turbulent Times

The Boys' School was divided into houses and in 1932 teacher Mr Barnett marked 25 years at the Boys' School by presenting a shield for house competitions. In April 1933 it was won by Dickens House, in 1934 by Nelson House. The other houses were Shakespeare and Haig and no doubt had their share of success too. In 1930 the Girls' School was also arranged into houses, named after four women; Johnson (aviator Amy), Nightingale (WW1 nurse Florence), Eliot (author George), and Anderson (Physician Dr Elizabeth G). Whether or not this was the first time such division had been arranged is unknown although it is the first mention of it in the logs.

In other less fortunate respects, the 1930s also seemed to be starting in the manner that the 1920s had ended. In 1930 the Infants' School Headmistress slipped and fractured her wrist in the school and, much worse, one of the Infant children died in the East Surrey Hospital after an operation. As had been the case for Gladys Terry, the school sent flowers and money. Heating, too remained a problem, as always, when on 9th January 1931 the temperature in juniors A form room in the Boys' School was 38°F and no boys were allowed in there until 9.50 am. In the following December a new heating system was installed and the old stoves removed.

An innovation of the late twenties and early thirties was that of talking films. The Picture Pavilion in Redhill had been converted in 1929 for the medium which was established in all local cinemas by 1933 when, on 17th June, *'The school saw and heard a 'talkie' film on wild animals in their nature haunts.'*

In August Headmaster Mr H.C.Cole finished officially at the school but stayed on for the prize-giving on 2nd September, which was held in the Parish Hall for the second year. The day before the prizes were distributed Mr Reginald George Bennett took over as the new Boys' School Head. One month later he bid farewell to the vicar, the Rev. Mannering, who was leaving for Bristol. In November the Armistice was marked in Church and officiated over by the incoming incumbent, the Rev S.G.Hooper.

Girls visited the Municipal Buildings, Fire Station and the Gas Works - as girls before them had done - and in 1933 a new boiler was installed (in the depths of winter as usual) and the school was very cold for a while. This was a time when the car had taken over considerably from the horse but the first mention of that vehicle's impact on normal life is in December 1933 when Infants' School teacher Miss Ariss was absent through injury following a car accident.

Boys' School staff members, classes and class sizes:			
Class	Teacher	Shared	On Roll
Standard 1	Miss Young		37
Standard 2	Mr Barnett		45
Standard 3	Mrs Mason		46
Standard 4	Mr Tarr		50
Standard 5	Mr Bradfield		46
Standard 6	Mrs Roopers [sic]	29	
Standard x7	Mr Bennett	20	49
Official accommodation 273		Total	273

Prize-giving this year ended with the school song, probably as it had on other occasions. When the school song was first sung (or last sung, for it is not used now) is unknown, but we do have the words, or at least two verses of them, courtesy of the memory of ex-pupil Reg. Harriden, and they are included later in this chapter.

In 1933 the boys retained the swimming shield. Here is an example of the failing of the logs, as it is not recorded as having been won the previous year, which it was. Obviously not everything can be recorded, but when it is not, information is lost, sometimes irretrievably. In March 1934 there is the first reference to the (then) recently built Redhill swimming baths, an alternative to the baths at Reigate used by the school for so long.

The 1932 swimming team with their success not yet written on the shield (and unrecorded in the school logbook). In the back row from l-r are Mr Tarr, K.Jordan, L.Dalton, V.Foot and Headmaster Mr Bennett. The boys sitting are M.Stapleton and S.Goldsmith. Foot and Stapleton went on to swim for Redhill Swimming Club.

Perhaps the new venue helped the boys again retain the swimming shield (for at least the third year in succession). The new baths reference was made two days before the opening of the also new South Park Junior School.

Fifteen girls attended an evening performance of Macbeth at the Old Vic on 20th April 1934. Three days later the timetable was altered to again hear details of an aviation triumph on the radio, this time the arrival in Melbourne of airmen Scott and Black who won the England-Melbourne race in one hour under three days. That first ever flight by Alan Cobham eight years before, the final part of which was listened to by girls at St John's in 1926, had taken four weeks and two days. The boys had the luxury of a cinema in one of their classrooms, that of Mr Tarr, and it is wondered if mention of installing a cinema in the basement of the Girls' School was ever acted upon. (More information on Mr Tarr's cinema appears later in this chapter).

On 30th October 1934 a new Honours Board was unveiled by Mrs A.W.Makovski and dedicated by the vicar, a deliberately impressive ceremony that the logs are silent about. As mentioned in chapter two, we can fairly safely surmise that it must have been to mark the 50th anniversary of the opening of the Boys' School building, and the date gives us an indication of the date of that ceremony, absent from 1884 records.

Royal Events

Royal events still featured strongly in the school year. In 1934 school closed all day on 28th November for the Duke of Kent's wedding to Princess Marina of Greece, and in 1935, May 6th and 7th were taken for children's celebrations connected with King George V Silver Jubilee. A memorial to this latter event stands on Redhill Top Common. It was created by converting an old brick column that was originally built as a sighting point for a long straight stretch of the 1840s Dover railway. Also in 1935 the school was closed for the wedding of the Duke of Gloucester to Princess Alice on 6th November at Westminster Abbey. King George V died at Sandringham on 20th January 1936, school closing for the funeral on the 28th. On 24th January some children were taken to the Memorial Sports Ground to hear the proclamation of King Edward VIII.

The possibility of the abdication of King Edward VIII because of his association with Mrs Simpson, a divorcée, was already known but a voluntary newspaper code of silence was adopted nationally, although details became known through the foreign press. The new King was to abdicate in order to marry Mrs Simpson and some children again went to the Sports Ground, this time to hear the proclamation of King George VI on 14th December 1936. The coronation was on 11th May and was celebrated in school by a pageant with the school closed on the day. On 29th May the girls went to the Majestic Cinema at Reigate to see the coronation film as guests of the Mayor.

In spite of time off being given for royal events, be they celebration or mourning, one small change creeping in during the 1930s was that there seemed to be fewer mentions of time off for some of the other once

In this old picture of Redhill Common the original sighting pillar can be seen far right on the site of the present memorial to King George V

traditional events, such as the flower shows and 5th November bonfire celebrations etc. Mention of the Farm School sports events and Harvest Homes had long since ended. Even the presence of a circus now only got school ending slightly earlier at 3.45 pm in the afternoon. However, the annual inter-school sports and school swimming galas still closed the schools for the day or afternoon as appropriate.

One thing that did not end was the occasional death of a child. An eight-year-old died in June 1935, the first mention of the death of a pupil since a boy died during the summer holidays of 1927 and the previously mentioned death of infant Gladys Terry in October 1929.

In May 1935, '*the Junior Boys were runners up, and the Senior Boys won the Challenge Shield at the school sports*'. If this means the inter-school sports then this is a slight change from previous logs which make no mention of sections or age differentials.

A Borough Education Committee minute of 5th July 1935 resolved that from the middle of November to the middle of January schools would adopt earlier hours, opening at 2 p.m. and closing at 4.05 p.m. Close of school was considerably later than those of previous years but possibly reflected the availability of public and other transport in use by this time. In December the school concert was held in the Central Hall as it had been in 1934. How many concerts there had been previously is unknown but the earliest noted in research was held at the Baptist Tabernacle at Redhill in 1924 under the Headship of Mr Oliver Gregson. The imprint Penguin Books was established in this year 1934, but ominously so was the Lüftwaffe.

In April 1936 Miss Davies, who only started in January as a teacher in the Infants' School was transferred to the new South Park Mixed School due to reduced numbers at St John's Infants'. These numbers were 108 (on books) which were re-organised from four to three classes. The Girls' School also lost a teacher. This year Joyce Payne was crowned May Queen at the School's May celebration, Empire Day was again celebrated at Mill Street, the fairly new Vicar left for Milford on Sea and a new man, the aptly named J.Ross MacVicar, took his place in time to officiate at the Church war memorial. On 16th November members of the Borough Education Committee came to look at the movable partition in one of the schools and one month later to the day there was that year's school concert.

Places visited in the second half of the decade included the Records Office in London, the

British Museum, Windsor Castle, the Royal School of Needlework, the open-air theatre in Regents Park and Kensington Palace. Children also saw television at the Science Museum on 12th June 1937. We might wonder how many of them were excited by the thought of how it might develop and affect their lives and how many simply accepted it for what it was and thought no more of it.

In the summer of 1937 the Infants' School Head reported that the shoes of the children from the Meadvale Home were too small. The Home's Matron called and went away promising to provide larger ones. Cracks appearing in the Infants' School ceilings were looked at by a surveyor and were to receive attention. The building was now 27 years old. Its predecessor was the subject of an old print that was cleaned and framed in June 1937 and presumably hung somewhere in the school. Whether it is the same one as hangs in the Head's office now is unknown, but it could possibly be judging from its frame. The picture of the original school at the front of this history is a copy of that print.

A new hot water system was installed in 1938. This year measles and chicken pox kept three-quarters of the children off school during March and April. Because so many were absent Miss Watson was sent on supply to Cromwell Road School. Miss Watson had been sick twice and on each occasion had been replaced by a Miss Datson.

In 1938 one of the girls, Joyce Whalebelly, presented a purse of £1.7.6 to HRH The Princess Alice, Countess of Athlone, money collected by St John's girls for the East Surrey Hospital. Harvest Festival had just been celebrated and some of the proceeds had been sent to that hospital, a tradition that went back many years. In 1930 two guineas had been collected by the school for the hospital and presented to HRH Princess Mary by pupil Elaine Terry.

In April 1939 the girls again won the Sports Shield and the boys won the Senior Shield the following month, apparently showing that boys and girls sports were held separately. Also in May 1939 the infants started listening to the 'rhythmic class broadcast' by the BBC. Tradition was broken on Empire Day by the three departments of the school gathering in their own playground rather than on the common to sing hymns and be addressed by Col. Spranger, Chairman of the Borough Education Committee, instead of the Mayor. Another new vicar, the Rev. Ball, had his feet under the vestry table by this time. In answer to the obvious question, he did go on to become Canon Ball. Appropriately his other initials were W.A.R.

Personal Memories of the 1930s

Mary Peters

Mary was at St John's from 1926-1934 and confirms that the uncertified teacher by the name of Whyman was the sister of the Headmistress of the same name. Miss Whyman lived in the big house on the end of Hillside Cottages, the row that is alongside the railings of the upper school playground. Another uncertified teacher she remembers was Miss Lee. Mr Tarr's cinema, mentioned earlier, was a lantern slide show that took place after school. Children had to pay a ha'penny or a penny to see it. She remembers hurrying home once to raid her money box for the required coin and getting into trouble from her parents afterwards for doing so. She felt aggrieved about this – after all, it was her money.

Continuing on the subject of films and 'talkies' the first talking picture she saw starred Janet Gaynor and Charles Farrell - she forgets the title - and she saw it at the Davis Theatre in Croydon. Closer to home she saw a silent film, Peter Pan, at the Reigate Hippodrome. Those were the days when the owners, Mr and Mrs Bancroft, attired in evening dress, greeted their patrons in the foyer, a pianist accompanied the film, and a commissionaire in full uniform sprayed the audience with rose scented water from time to time during the performance.

Mary points out that the Workhouse was also known as the 'Union'. This was because it had been created by a number of parishes (or a union) getting together to build and finance it. The Workhouse provided temporary shelter for vagrants (also referred to later in Bertie House's reminiscences) who were provided with a ration of tea when they left to go on their way. They would call at local houses for hot water and perhaps something to eat.

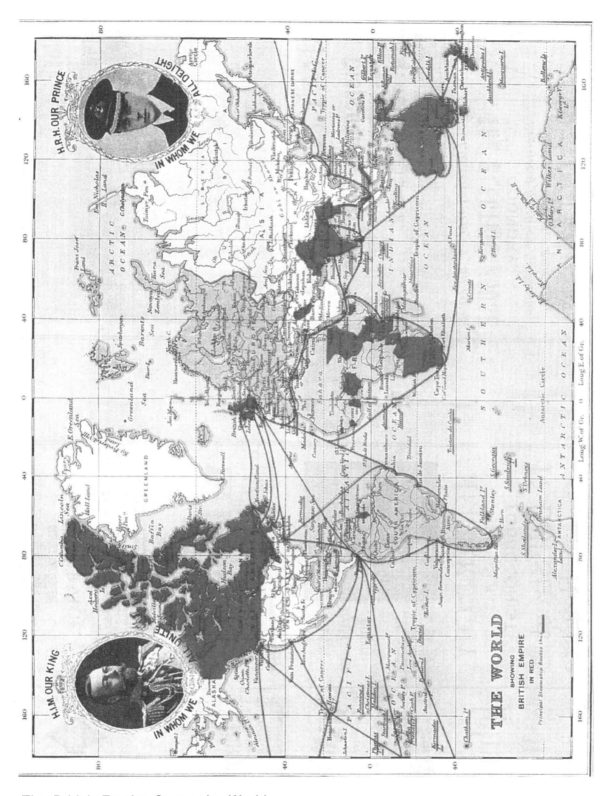

The British Empire Spans the World
A 1926 poster of the British Empire, a celebration of which was held annually at St John's School during much of the first five decades of the 19th century. Inset show King George V, whose first 25 years on the throne are celebrated by the monument on the Top Common, and his son, Prince Edward.

The School on the Common

Another of her memories is of 'big' weddings at St John's Church, when the carpet and awnings were brought out. They stretched from the church porch to the bottom of the steps where cars would be waiting. The gentlemen wore morning dress and the ladies pretty dresses and high heeled shoes. The ladies had to be heavily supported down the slope on the slippery carpet. All this was duly noted by the local children waiting at the bottom.

The church was always full in those days - at least for morning services - and Mary remembers that some people still had their names on little brass plates attached to the pews. Sunday School was held in the Boys' School, which belonged to the church, the Superintendent being Mrs Margaret Knight. The great event of the year was the Sunday School outing, if you attended regularly you could go for 6d. There was great excitement as mothers went too on a train from Earlswood station, and for many children this was their only outing to the sea.

Mary remembers the shops at St John's as Pattenden's and Terry's. Mrs Terry would sell the children a farthing's worth of sweets. Two other people sold vegetables from their cottages,

Mary Peters appears in the following photo circa.1933, she is second from right in the third row back. The classroom is the one looking out onto the girls' playground. The two large pictures on the wall are perhaps among those presented by visiting dignitaries on Empire Days and other occasions. Formal school wear seems to have been adopted by about half the girls, who were not usually this crowded together but have moved to one side of the room to all get in shot. From right to left:

Front Row Freda Walworth - unknown - Elizabeth Hunter - Muriel Roberts - unknown - Yvonne Baldwin
Row 2 Paddy Worth - unknown -? Terry (one of twins in the class) - unknown - ? Hill - Gladys Waite - Mary Palmer - Hilda Holder
Row 3 Nellie ? - Mary Peters - Betty Jardine - Molly Brown - Edna ? - Mollie Sparks
Row 4 Joan Bryant - unknown -Doris Hyder - Margaret Hewitt - unknown - unknown
Row 5 ? Terry (other twin) - Joyce Foot - Winnie Procter - unknown - unknown - unknown
Standing unknown - unknown - ? Smith (parents had the Ship Pub) - unknown - Gladys Hill - Ethel ? - Ida Stanley (father was chauffeur at The Mount) - Ethel Upfold, unknown, unknown.
Picture kindly supplied by Mary Peters.

another lady made toffee apples and an old man made ginger beer. On hot Sundays Mr Tom Piggott, who owned the sweet shop near the Plough public house, made ice cream which he served from a bowl. There was a boot repairer and two general handymen, Mr Gear and Mr Willett. Mr Gear also did funerals, assisted by his brother, Arthur, and Mr Hall the boot repairer. Mary remembers seeing Mr Gear with a small coffin tucked under his arm. She wonders if he was taking it to the Workhouse for a tiny child.

Mary also lived in Hillside Cottages, and when returning home along Kings Avenue at night would always run past the derelict Brickmakers Arms public house because she thought it might be haunted. The area had two brickworks, one by the lower of the two Earlswood lakes and one at Meadvale. Incidentally, Kings Avenue was sometimes called Sandy Lane because it was not made up. Mary believes the name Kings Avenue derives from a Mr King who once lived at the end of Carters Cottages and made brooms for the crossing sweepers in London, the material required being always at hand nearby.

The common was well-kept, with a man who picked up litter with a spiked stick and a common-keeper, Mr Hewett, who was the bane of the children's lives - or was that the other way around? Mary thinks that the children of St John's led very happy lives because they had the whole of the common to play on in an age when there were fewer people about and far less traffic.

The laundry was a thriving place and provided work for many local people over the years, often for more than one generation. In the hot weather the big doors opposite the school were thrown open and the women could be seen doing the hand-washing at great long sinks and ironing the more delicate things. The vans were busy all day long bringing in parcels and big wickerwork hampers. Even ordinary households were able to send father's stiff white collars, the best sheets and the white linen tablecloths.

John Woods

Ex-pupil Mr John Woods remembers St John's Boys' School in the early 1930s when the Head was Mr Bennett and the teachers were Mrs Young, Mr Barnett, Mr Tarr, Mrs Mason and Mr Bradfield. The Central Hall in London Road, Redhill was brand new in 1934 and that same December was the venue for a concert held by St John's boys. Mr Woods, who was one of the fiddlers still has the printed programme and many names of past pupils appear on its pages. Incidentally Mr Woods recalls that when he got the cane from Mr Bennett he was allowed to choose either the thick end or the thin end but was never sure which was the best choice as both hurt equally. When he and a friend discovered that choirboys were paid they presented themselves for the singing test. The choirmaster, nicknamed 'Beaky' because of the size of his nose, put them through the test and passed them, but only for filling-in when other choirboys were unavailable. The top rate for the job was 7/6d and John and his friend received 6d, both rates payable three-monthly.

Reg Harriden

Reg Harriden

More details are recalled by Reg, who left St John's in 1937. His memory of the Girls' School is of Miss White taking over from Miss Towell as the head in 1936 or 7 and of teachers being Misses Schmidt, Lees, Sandys, Barber and Griffin. He remembers also Miss Whyman as head of the Infants' and Miss Cross as a teacher there. The Boys' School had Mr Bennett as Head, and teachers, Mrs Young (class 1), Mr Barnett (class 2), Mr Jones (class 3), Mr Mole (class 4), Mr Bradfield (class 5) and Mr Tarr (class 6). Bennett, Barnett and Jones, he recalls, were members of the church choir. The building was divided into six classrooms with cloakrooms at each end. Three of the classrooms became the hall when the screens were withdrawn for assembly. At Hooley School in St John's Road were some single storey buildings where the girls went for laundry and cooking lessons

The School on the Common

Reg features centre of a photo taken in 1931 or 32 by a teacher who wanted to try out a new camera. The boys are standing by the boys' playground on the ground between the school and the laundry. From left to right they are Ken Morgan, Derek Hodder, Reg Harriden, Eric Edwards and Reg Norman.

once a week (a brief Girls' School log entry of 14th June 1927, *'Cookery girls attended the new centre'*, might be a reference to the first use of this facility) and the boys went for woodwork under Mr Bamforth.

The 'marathon' run, actually about four miles, was up onto Redhill Top Common, along High Trees Road and through the pinewoods to Smoke Lane. From there the route continued down Cockshot Hill to the Angel, around the corner into the farmyard, now the site of a small shopping centre and the Woodhatch Community Centre, along footpaths across what is now the Woodhatch estate to Meadvale, then through the passage ways passing close by the Mount back to St John's School.

A small coincidence during the writing of this history was that the first reference to the school song was noted on 2nd May 2000 during research at the Woking History Centre. 1940s ex-Boys' School Teacher, Miss Worcester, was contacted but was unable to throw any light upon what it might have been. The very next day, 3rd May, a letter from Mr Harriden arrived not only referring to that very song but detailing the words: -

We will remember in the years to be
All we were hoping, all our longing here,
And in that corner of our memory
Fond recollections will be doubly clear.

So when we look back in the years ahead,
Objectives gained, our strivings understood,
We'll turn to you, who showed the path to tread.
We will remember with gratitude.

Reg says that he does not know the origin of the song, so we may never know the author, which is a shame. Its words and sentiment are strong and emotive, especially when looked back upon with the experience of a life built upon the learning acquired from St John's School days. But for Mr Harriden's strong recollection of 70 years ago they might have been completely lost to us. He says in his letter that he was privileged to win the 'Most Worthy Boy' award of 1937, a bible which he still has. When he also says that he can still recall the tune to which these words are set it seems that 'Most Worthy' is an apt title to which he was justly entitled.

Mr Harriden's son went to the new Sandcross Lane School when St John's Boys moved there, and in 1963 or 64 was awarded the school prize still known as the 'Barnett Prize'.

Mr Harriden has been married for 53 years, at the time of writing, to Joyce Whalebelly, who presented the purse to HRH Princess Royal, the Princess Alice, Countess of Athlone, in 1938 (see text for that period) and in the St John's concert programme for 1934, Reg's name is to be found. He was also a member of the St John's scout troop.

Diana Moore

Diana has lived at Carters Cottages from the age of six months and has seen many changes there and at the school. She was also a pupil in the 1930s and, although she did not have a picture of herself at St John's she kindly provided one of her brother's 1930s class, shown here. She also brought a point to mind that had not before surfaced: the possible toot of a coach-horn has been mentioned, as has the gasworks hooter, but Diana remembered that there was one much closer to the school, at the laundry. It sounded at 12 pm and 5 pm and possibly other times as well. The probability was that most of the workers there lived very close by and would know when to start and stop work by its note.

Another 1930s classroom, the first on the left inside the Infants' entrance. According to the card on the desk at bottom right of picture is class 1A Front row: Georgie Withers, Beryl? Moody, rest unknown. 2nd row; 4 unknowns, Dorothy? Kingsnorth, Fred Seldon? 3rd row: Elaine Dando, John Moore, Joyce Kearn, Eric? Pearman, Dorothy Kingsnorth, ? Lashmar. Back row: All unknown. Standing along left wall: Unknown, Edwina? Roffey, unknown, Stanley Howick, Yvonne Puddy? Standing along back wall: Ronald Terry, unknown, Henry Smith, unknown, unknown.

Bertie House's Reminiscences

My father Harold, his two brothers and three sisters, all started their education during the 1890s and 1900s at 20 Somerset Road, one of Meadvale's three schools, which in 1884 came under the same management as St John's School. Teachers at number 20 during this period included Mrs Robinson, Miss Peat and my great aunt, Miss Rose Gallard. After infancy schooling at Meadvale, children would transfer to St John's.

My Aunt Doris House was in the Girls' School in 1905 with teachers Miss Harriden and Miss Thorpe. The former lived at St John's and her brother was a bootmaker. Auntie Doll was considered to be a good buttonholer and was chosen to make the buttonholes in a pair of knickers being made for the Head Mistress, Miss Lansdell. Buttons were used in those days because the garment had plackets at each side of the front and back waistbands that were secured by buttons.

My stepfather-in-law, William Charles Brown, born in 1879, was one of the first boys in the Boys' School, built in 1884. After leaving he was apprenticed to master-builder Mr W Bagaley of Meadvale, Mayor of Reigate 1893-95. William later became a well-known builder.

William married but sadly his first born son, Frank, died from typhoid fever aged 13 months on the same day that

Children and staff of Meadvale School in 1906. Miss Robinson (head) is on the left and teacher Miss Rose Gallard is on the right. Second child from the right in the row next to back is Dora House. Picture courtesy of Bertie House

Children and staff of Meadvale School in 1912.
From l-r Back row: - Miss Peat - ? Buckell - Wally Best - Dick Woodman - George Burberry - unknown -Willie Walker - unknown. Row 2: - Emily Wilshire - unknown - unknown - ? Terry - unknown - Violet Shorter - Steve Warren - Maggie Pearce - Bill Pilbeam - unknown - Mrs Robinson (Head). Row 3 - Amy Brewer - Ede Terry - unknown - Hilda House - unknown - unknown - unknown - Rosie Adams - Miriam Barnes - unknown. Front row: - Doris Long - Bill Brown - unknown - Billy Elliot - Grace Hewitt - Ivy Payne - Vera Parker. Picture courtesy Bertie House

Children in the Mount pathways that lead from Meadvale to St John's. Bertie's father is the boy 2nd from the left in the left-hand group. His Aunt Doll is 2nd from the right in the same group. 2nd from left in the right-hand group is Harry Broomer, whose father looked after the beagles that belonged to Mr Hayward at Woodhatch House. Picture courtesy Bertie House

Another of Bertie's aunts, Kathleen House, was Head Girl in 1910 when she was presented with a silver medal. She was Head Girl again in 1911 when she was given a prayer book. The front and reverse sides of the Head Girl's medal are shown here. Pictures courtesy Bertie House

William Charles Brown is 4th from left in the back row in this 1889 group. On the right is Head Master Mr Jinks, who first came to St John's in 1876 and was to remain until 1919. Picture courtesy Bertie House

Bertie's class , 1932. From left to right the boys are : -
Back row - Brian Day - Paul Jardine - Billy Hazelgrove - ? Allen - Roger Hodder - Doug powell - Tim Copus - Stanley Seldon - Reggie Bryant. Centre row - Kem Marlow - Ron Day - Alan Peters - Eric Langridge - Jumbo Smith - unknown - unknown - Dave Saunders - Reggie Norman - Lionel Dulake. Front row - J Parker - ? Hemsley - Joe Maskell - Tommy Lashmar - Roy Allman - Derek Cook - Micky Cornish - Bertie House - Sid Penton - Maurice Pink - Alfie Forrest - Stanley Crocker. Picture courtesy Bertie House

Empire Day 1911. Bertie's Aunt Kath House is 6th from the left in the middle row. Picture courtesy Bertie House

The School on the Common

Ellen, his second child, was born. He had two more children, Minnie and Ronald, and all three attended St John's (Ellen appears in the 1917-1918 picture of children posing around a maypole in ch6). Minnie married the Rev. Muzio, a curate at St John's Church 1933-1934. Ron was awarded a prize for general intelligence in form 1 in 1927 and won the scooter and fairy cycle race in 1928.

My own association with the school began in 1928 when I joined the Infants' School and started using a counting frame, modeling clay and a slate board. Infant boys and girls were taught together in classrooms adjoining the Girls' School, as they are today, with Miss Whyman as Head Mistress.

Boys' School followed, with teachers Mrs Young in Standard 1, Miss Barnet 2, Miss Mason 3, Mr Bradfield 4, Mr Tarr 5 and Mr Bennett, Head Master, conducting Standard 6, consisting of four to six advanced pupils, in his front lobby. Mrs Young initiated boys into the repetitive chanting method of learning multiplication tables, which is something I have found of lifelong benefit. Youngsters today use calculators, even in exams.

I remembers Mr Barnett as a strict and stern faced teacher who was well suited to adjudicating at the sports day races held annually at the Ring on Earlswood Common. Miss Mason was keen on using her knuckle-rapping ruler and 'clipping one's ear' with her hand - plus its gold ring! Mr Bradfield was a kind and gentle teacher but a little hard of hearing. Mr Fred Tarr was totally different; he was the youngest teacher in the school, was energetic and a good sports controller but very unforgiving to classroom sweet eaters and talking, so was enthusiastic with his long cane. Depending on how many strokes of the cane had been administered - six was usually the maximum - the hand-stinging sensation could last up to half an hour. Persistent offenders were paraded through to the Head Master's room (the lobby inside the school entrance) where he would treat them to 'six of the best'. I have often wondered if the Standard 6 pupils who were in the lobby were forced to watch such punishment or asked to avert their eyes or leave the room.

Ernest 'Sos' Clayton, a school monitor and the tallest boy in the school, was a member of Standard 6. One of his duties was to record the classroom temperatures from thermometers suspended from the ceilings throughout the school - I often wondered if he got the job because he was the most able to reach and read the thermometer scales. It should be recorded that Ernie's persistence with an earlier St John's Head Master, Mr H Cole, resulted in a scout group being formed at the school in 1930. I and many others were very grateful for his efforts.

Along with many other children living in Meadvale, I used to walk to school twice each day through Mount Walk and past the Hygienic Laundry (now the site of Ardshiel Drive). In winter a boy could stand by the sulphurous slag piles outside its boiler house and sneak a warming from its roaring boilers when Mr Clutterbuck, the laundry engineer, was not about. In the summer, when the laundry doors were open, the laundering operations being carried out could be seen; all very exciting for young boys! When approaching school and after lunch the bell of the school clock was tolled to give a distant warning to potential latecomers. Miss Mary Peters remembers ringing it during the mid-1930s, when she was a senior pupil, by pulling on a rope extending down into a classroom.

The Boys' School was divided into houses, with Dickens (blue), Shakespeare (yellow), Nelson (red) and Haig (green), presumably to promote a more competitive atmosphere in school events. Coloured lapel badges were generally worn but for playground activities, such as physical training exercises, drill and organised games, coloured braiding circlets were worn over one shoulder and the opposite arm.

Mr Tarr looked after the sports activities. During playtime he would play cricket outside the playground where an old tree stump would be used as a single wicket. Inter-school matches were played at the Ring on Earlswood Common. I remember that Fred Weller was a very good bowler. Inter-school football matches were played on a pitch adjacent to the Ring with Mr Tarr acting as referee. In 1936 he selected Micky Cornish and myself to go for a trial to play in the Borough School Team. Alas, it rained on the due Saturday morning and my mother would not let me go. Several years later, when I was playing cricket for Meadvale, Ralph West, the organiser, who was supervisor at Brown's Brickyard in Meadvale, arranged for me to have a trial for the Surrey Colts Cricket Team, but when my mother found out it was on a Sunday I was forbidden to attend and that

George Bundell won the Victor Ludorum (Hull) Cup for the most points gained in the 1932 Sports day, and is pictured here with other prizewinners. Back row - unknown - Ken Jordan - Eric Maxwell - Alf Jackson - unknown - Eric? Swan - unknown - Derek Hodder - Teacher Mr Tarr - Roy Allman - unknown - Roy Swetman.
2nd row - Huby Day - Bub Dalton - Frank Weller - Billy Ellwood - Roger Hodder - Steve List - unknown - Alan Parker - Steve Jackson - unknown - Peter Thompson - unknown.
3rd row - Doug Powell - unknown - unknown - ? Moody - Ronnie Hoppr - George Bundell (with cup) - rest unknown.
Front row - unkown (half hidden) - unknown - unknown - Derek Cook - Percy Cook - Merlin Howell - Stanley Crocker - unknown. Picture courtesy Bertie House

chance was also lost. How times have changed!

The annual school sports were always held at the Ring and I never remember it raining for the event. Sports days would not have been complete without the presence of James (Jock) Robinson, a local policeman who lived in Brambletye Park Road. He was a jovial character who enjoyed a good relationship with children and the general public. I sampled his humour in 1932 after winning the sack race when he held up my sack to the spectators, emphasising its size. It was actually the type known as a 'poke', which was wide enough for me almost to run in with my feet tucked well into each corner. Star performers in my time included Peter Wakeman, Dennis Cornish and George Bundell.

Apart from his prowess on sports day, Den Cornish also won the cross country race (inaugurated 1926 and route previously described) on two occasions. Dennis went on to play Athenian League football for Redhill and Southall for many years.

Peter Wakeman leapt to four feet nine inches, winning the high jump event at the Ring in the mid-1930s. After winning the same event in the Borough School Sports he went on to represent Surrey in the All England Schools Championships held at Brighton and finished third with a jump of five feet one inch.

St John's boys seem always to have enjoyed their swimming, for between 1911 and 1932 they won the local Schools Championships on eight occasions. They were, however, surpassed by Holmesdale School, which won 11 times - but they no doubt benefited by having the Reigate baths so close to their school. Redhill swimming baths were not built until 1934 and from then on St John's Boys used to march down to Redhill for their weekly swimming lessons. I learnt to swim this way, always enjoying a penny bar of Nestles chocolate from the dispensing machine in the baths on the way back to school. A picture of the 1932 swimming team appears earlier in this chapter.

Not all of Mr Tarr's energy was expended during school hours, after lessons we could stay on and attend his 'cinema show', when black and white films of the Charlie Chaplin era were shown from the clattering projector. He also sold short lengths of 35mm film that were taken home and run through toy hand-cranked machines onto a wall or white sheet. We soon found out that the film material was highly inflammable and could be easily ignited by the sun's rays through a magnifying glass.

Weekly Young People's Union meetings, under the leadership of Miss Fyson, were held in Meadvale Hall where boys made wooden framed stools with woven sea-grass seats. Mr Tarr and the curates from St John's Church were sometimes visitors to the meetings when the handiwork would be inspected.

During my days there were no dining facilities at school and most boys went home for lunch. In the mid-1930s school milk was introduced Roy Allman and myself were the first boys to take it. The milk, in a one-third-pint bottle with a cardboard disc top and a push-out piece to accept a straw, was drunk during morning playtime. I think the cost was a halfpenny a bottle.

Tramps were often seen in the late afternoons of the winter months in Union Road (now Pendleton Road) approaching the workhouse (where St John's Park is now) so that they could spend the night under cover, and do so free if they were penniless. Before they entered the workhouse those with odd pennies to hide would bury them by the side of the high brick wall (still standing) that surrounded the site, not realising that they were being watched by eagle-eyed boys on their way home from school. As soon as the tramps went inside the boys would 'home in' to dig up the 'hidden treasure'.

When I left St John's in 1936 to go to the Redhill Junior Technical School I did not imagine visiting St John's again, but in 1976, following retirement, I took on the job of winding and servicing the school clock. I gained much pleasure and satisfaction in visiting the school twice weekly and was very disappointed in 1999 to learn the Health and Safety Regulations would prohibit me from scaling the heights in the school tower. Since then discussions have taken place resulting in the School Governors agreeing to the replacement of the present mechanical movement with a radio-controlled clock which would involve the very minimum of labour. (There is more about the clock in Chapter 12).

In 1986 a third generation attendee at St John's was my grandson. He was not there long as the family moved away.

Peter Wakeman

Mentioned in Bertie House's reminiscences, Peter made a couple of interesting additions to this and preceding chapters when recalling St John's in the 1930s. The first was to remember another teacher not previously recorded. This was 'Hitler' Hopkins, a replacement in the Boys' School, he thinks, for Mrs Mason, and whose nickname reflected his disciplinary actions with the cane.

The other was that Bertram Mills Circus would unload elephants and ponies at the Redhill railway station and walk them up to Pickfords' yard in Brighton Road where they would remain until the circus had been set up on the common and they could be transferred there. This would be a treat for local children who would have two opportunities to see the circus animals on the streets - one before the circus began, and another when the circus packed up and moved on.

Chapter Eight
The Nineteen-forties

World War Two

The outbreak of war delayed the return of children to school after the summer holidays in 1939 because the air raid shelters were not ready. The staff returned on the allotted day of 5th September and were kept busy assisting in the billeting of children evacuated from London and a scheme to keep in touch with their own pupils during the closure. The staff of the Girls' School decided to visit children at their homes to set and mark work. On 18th September school resumed. Instruction was only provided to one fifth of the children each day, either in the morning or the afternoon because other schools were also using the building. The London school was using part of the upper building on the other half days and children evacuated from Croydon also arrived and joined the London school. Altogether four other schools were using the premises. Overcrowding and 'shift' working were inevitable with the use of the Meadvale Adult School hall and Elim hall being used by the Girls' School, 50 girls at a time. The effect was to reduce classes to 45 minutes instruction in any one session.

The Boys' School was in a similar situation, with a school from Sydenham sharing its facilities. It re-opened after the summer break on 30th October for those whose parents gave written permission. Only half of each day was spent fully by the boys in their own building. The other half was spent by some in one room while the others were spread between the Parochial Hall, the Meadvale Hall, the school garden at Fairlawn, in the playground or on the common for games. These arrangements alternated a.m./p.m. between the two sharing schools.

Fewer mentions of diphtheria appear in the school logs but it was still around, as one infant was

excluded in January of 1940 for having had contact with a case of the disease. Any infection could easily be spread among very many children when on occasions such as Empire Day, the combined numbers of St

An Anderson shelter, the kind that some children might have had in their gardens for use during air raids out of school hours. This picture is of a full size model made for a 1994 exhibition at the Reigate Priory Museum and is reproduced courtesy of the Museum.

The School on the Common

John's Boys', St John's Girls', St John's Infants, Dalmain Road Juniors, Dalmain Road Infants, Kilmonie LCC, Ecclesbourne Senior Girls' and Banstead Girls' Schools were all gathered together.

Ecclesbourne Girls' moved to Reigate at the end of February 1940, freeing one classroom for the Girls, and a second one was freed in April 1940, allowing St John's Girls' School three classrooms and partial use of the hall. At this time the Head Mistress returned after three months' absence following an operation. By 15th May a Banstead school was in one Girls' classroom and desks were put into the playground in dry weather. As stated above, Empire Day was celebrated by the whole school plus the evacuated schools together. The next day there was practice in use of the air raid shelters and getting out of them via the manholes. It is more than possible that at this time some of the children were having a whale of a time even if the staff were not.

The 1940 Whitsun holiday was cancelled and children returned to school after only one week off. Many of the outside activities that attracted children away from school in the past had ended. An exception was Sunday school excursions to the coast, the school being closed for just such an event on June 26th 1940. This is surprising in view of the shortened Whitsun holiday, a war in progress and restrictions on large gatherings. The effect of the 'phoney war', that period when the expected attacks on cities had not materialised, resulted in some evacuated children returning to London and previously closed cinemas being re-opened, and may have contributed to relaxed attitudes on the matter. However, only one day earlier, through the previous night and early hours of the morning of the 25th, there had been air raid alerts. As a consequence children were allowed a half-hour rest before commencing work.

This quiet period of the 'phoney war' was interrupted on 16th July when the children had to go to air raid shelters after heavy firing had been heard. On 15th August they were there again due to an air raid alert. There were two more alerts the following day and thereafter

The half-round basement window was originally the only one, the others being added when the basement was converted to a classroom in 1940.

the children spent considerable time in the shelters. After night raids the school would sometimes remain closed the following morning. Attempts to continue lessons in the shelters were difficult but when more time was spent in the shelters than out of them, teachers and children must have got used to the situation to some extent. Whether anyone got used to the overcrowding in the buildings is unlikely, with two classrooms in the Girls' School still being taken by other schools and part of the basement being converted to a classroom, with whitewashed walls and extra windows put in.

Miss Sadler of the Girls' School got married at the end of June. She had been Mrs Lewis for less than two months when the first bombs, 125 of them, fell on the Borough on the evening of 15th August 1940. Apart from three cyclists being knocked off their machines, no one was hurt. Three days later 5 people were killed and six injured by a bomb dropped at Shaws Corner. Other bombs were dropped at various times during the ensuing month with windows being smashed at Frenches Road School but no one there was hurt, although people were injured in Reigate and at Hardwick Road, Meadvale, not far from St John's. A bomb on the common south of the school completely severed the main Redhill outfall sewer.

On 29th August a Borough Education Committee ruling stated that if air raid alerts finished before midnight the school was to open at 10 am but if the all clear was not given until after midnight then the school stayed closed in the morning. Immediately after this almost two complete pages of school logs are filled with notes of the school closed or, when open, with nothing but air raid alerts and the children going into the shelters. On 14th September 1940 the ruling was amended so schools opened at 9am in the case of pre-midnight all clears, and at 10am when all clears did not sound until after midnight.

Incidentally, the siren used to sound the beginning and end of alerts was situated on the top of the Co-op in Redhill. It was perfectly audible on the town side of the common and presumably also on the other side. There was also a siren on top of the fire tower at the Municipal Buildings in Reigate and, it is believed, at Prince Albert Square at Salfords.

A log entry of the 4th October 1940 records, *'Raid warnings from 12.5 to 5.40. Children in shelters - about 50 children had to remain without lunch. Head Mistress bought loaves, jam & margarine, but was only able to allow one thick slice per child.'* The next day the children were in the shelters from 9.50 to 11.15, from 1.30 to 2.30 and 3.50 to 5.10. Clearly there could be problems in getting children home, and another getting them to school in the first place, as once they set out there was no shelter to run to in the case of a raid until they got to school. Buses were proposed for those from Salfords and South Park but whether they were laid on is unknown.

Another problem was with the shelters themselves, school logs noting, *'Shelters are in an exceedingly wet condition - walls are streaming and water dropping from roof continuously. Several children and staff are suffering from sore throats and colds in consequence'.*

Raids continued in October with damage in various parts of the Borough. On the 27th six people were killed and five injured in Emlyn Road, Redhill. On the 28th the London School, Dalmain Road Infants', was officially merged with St John's and the first Assistant Teacher, Miss Howes, became a member of the staff, although still paid by the LCC. She had charge of the 3rd class in the old babies' room and Miss Islip had the smallest children in the staff room. The staff room was one of the upper rooms in the upper building, probably at the south end as it is the largest. Evidence for this is that in 1943 HM Inspector had the London evacuees moved into the staff room and St John's own babies moved downstairs into another class. Classrooms II and III were given to Dalmain Road School and St John's own class II was in the hall. That day there were two air raid alerts, the next there were three. Exams were taken in the girls' basement, now converted to an emergency classroom, and the relegation of the marking of Armistice Day from a two minute silence to a mention at assembly probably means that 1938 was possibly the last time the two minute silence was observed at St John's.

It is said that air raid practice was carried out each day but often the shelters were used in earnest, presumably obviating the need for a practice. On 20th November 1940 the shortening of

The St John's football team of 1938 - kindly lent by Mr H.S.Day, who names the players as -
Rear:- M Cornish, F Weller, T Copus
Centre:- P Robinson, D Saunders, D Hemsley
Front:- J Moody, V Noris, H S Day, I Evans, D Mole

the afternoon for the children to leave early at 3.30 p.m. began as it had ever since it was started in 1914 to reflect the presence of billeted troops and the darkened streets. The reason now was so the children could get home before the blackout began. From 25th November the children started leaving even earlier at 2.45pm. Unfortunately the school itself had no means of blackout so presumably the staff also left before lights were needed. This also meant no Christmas party for the infants this year.

Everyone was affected by the war; many had relatives directly involved. Headmaster Mr Bennett's son was on military service in Ireland, Mr Bennett taking leave of absence on 25th April 1940 to see him off. Teacher Mr Mole was absent in October due to the death of his son, although the circumstances are not revealed in the logs. Additional information is given by the 28th October entry, *'Funeral of Mr Mole's son who had been school captain'.* Bombs continued to fall. Evacuation to the Borough was not safe enough for two 16 year-olds evacuated from St Dunstans to Hethersett at Reigate; they were killed on 5th November. An eleven-year-old boy, also from St Dunstans, was killed whilst out walking in February 1941. Ten people were killed and over a dozen injured by a parachute mine at South Merstham in April of 1941.

Two teachers from the Boys' School, Mr Tarr and Mr Bradfield, left in January and April respectively, to become heads of schools in Somerset. Mr Tarr, who lived in Somerset Road, Meadvale, had started at St John's in the middle of July 1927 so was ending an association of almost fourteen years with the school. By May 1941 there were 184 on role in the Infants School, and Empire Day was celebrated as usual by the whole school on 23rd May. At the end of August teacher Mrs Young left after 34 years at the school.

In April 1941 four managers came to inspect the Boys' School shelters, but not for any of the reasons one might expect. The boys had decorated the walls with colourful paintings of Snow White and the Seven Dwarfs, Robinson Crusoe, Regin the Dwarf, Robin Hood and many other story-book characters. The Manager's report gave the area painted as 300 feet long with an average depth of four feet - 1,200 square feet in all - an indication of the size of the shelters. At the time two walls remained unpainted, being reserved for Treasure Island and Pilgrims Progress. The news of the paintings spread. They were filmed by Pathé News and photographed by Fox Photos in the July. The shelters were closed after the war, only being re-opened in 2003. There is more about the shelters in chapter 12.

Reminiscences

David Parsons
David was a pupil during 1939-45 and remembers the air raid shelters well, especially the smell of dampness and the titles of the books he read in them when there were no lessons. Black Beauty, Gulliver's Travels, Lilliput, King Arthur, all passed his time during air alerts. Each Friday children were checked to see they had their gas masks and the two bars of chocolate kept in them, rations sufficient to sustain a child for two days in a shelter if necessary. And he tells of diving over a low brick wall in St John's Road when, on his way home from St John's School with his brother, a lone German aeroplane strafed the area with machine gun fire. (Two other reports of similar incidents, one in Reigate Priory and another in Reigate High Street, might all be part of the same single incident.)

He remembers using a slate in the Infants' School with a slate pencil tied to one corner of its wooden frame by string. Mr Weeds, a Boys' School Teacher, smoked a pipe, lighting it with a flip-top lighter that he failed to extinguish properly one day, setting his jacket alight in class. David says he got the cane from Mr Weeds once, even though he was not the headmaster. The cane broke and David got a splinter in his hand that turned septic. He says that there was hell to pay, with his father going to the school to complain.

Other teachers he remembers are Mr Mole, who used to organise tobogganing on the common in the winter, and Mr Nicholson, who rode a bike with the saddle so far tipped back he always wondered how he stayed on it.

Ray Best

Ray left Alexander Road Primary School in 1943 and started at St John's Boys' School in Standard V under Mr Nicholas *('pork pie hat, gammy leg and quite a good artist')*. He went to Standard 6 with Mr Ross and Standard 7 and 7x with Mr Mole. He remembers the boys used to chat to the laundry girls by the ever-open doors of the laundry. He also remembers going to the Elm Shades to buy the Head, Mr Bennett (nicknamed 'Glowgy' or 'Glogie') an arrowroot biscuit, and to Mrs Attwood's shop for twenty Churchmans cigarettes, during playtime.

St John's pigeons were delicious roasted, he says. Mr Peat, the caretaker, a friend of his father, had the job of cleaning up after the pigeons roosting on the roof vents in the upper building. In the 1950s he asked David's' father, a pigeon fancier, if he wanted to come and get some after school, which he did, taking David along. They were on several occasions able to collect pigeons from the roof, return some ringed ones to their owners, use some for breeding and others for the pot.

School Affairs - the War continues

A sad event was the death of pupil Michael Dean. On 19th November 1941 he fell from his cycle during the midday break and struck his head on a tree. The accident happened close to school and first aid was rendered by Mr Bennett but it would seem that the blow was beyond first aid, as Michael died the following day.

This was the year when permission was given for all the unused reading books to go for salvage for the war effort, and also when a group consisting of members of the Borough Education Committee, Borough Councillors, School Managers and the Borough Surveyor came to consider plans to start a canteen for which 330 children had already been nominated to receive school dinners.

Mr Jones of the Boys' School was called up for military service on 5th January 1942 and infants brought £13.4.6d to school for Warship Week, the older girls having deposited £223.2.0 in National Savings. Miss Woolley started as an extra teacher in the Infants' School on 4th May to take Miss Islip's place when she left in the summer. Miss Jones took a day off as it was the last day of her son's embarkation leave; Empire Day was celebrated in the playground; Dr Patterson came to examine children because scarlet fever was about, and *'seven ARP men came to examine the children's gas masks'.* Miss Islip left the Infants' School and was presented with a handbag, and Miss Howes was withdrawn as the number of evacuee children had dropped to a very low level. She was presented with a tea tray. In the Boys' School there was so much sickness amongst the teaching staff that it was April 13th before all were present at once.

For the first time the school was open during the summer holidays for activities, although numbers attending varied between only five and twelve infants and none of the older boys or girls at all. Out of the 33 daily bottles of milk in the Infants' School at least 21 went unclaimed. This exercise seems not to have been repeated for obvious reasons and ran the risk of over-working

Boys' School staff of the 1940s
Back Row: L-R: - Mrs Nicholas,
Mr Mole, Mr Weeds, Mr Ross,
Mr Jones, Miss Willett
Front: Mrs Bonner, Mr Bennett
(Headmaster), Miss Worcester

teachers (presuming it was teachers who staffed the school during the holiday). Miss Woolley was doing fire guard as well as teaching, an added duty that left her so worn out she was unable to teach by the December. No bombs fell on the Borough that year and there were only 20 alerts. Everything was normal, or as close as it could get to that balmy condition in the middle of a war.

In May Mr Barnett left after 35 years at the Boys' School, and Mr Allen left to be Head of an Oxfordshire school. It seems that a great deal of experience was being lost to St John's at this time, but then this is no doubt the case for all schools from time to time, and life goes on. Mr Ross and Mr Weeds, neither of them novices, filled the gaps.

In the Infants' School Miss Worcester, a supply teacher, took charge of class IV for the first month of 1943 and they lent her to the Boys' School to cover the absence of Mrs Nicholas. A small coincidence here - actually a very large coincidence - is that both these teachers lived in the same road in Merstham, and these words were written in the very same house as Miss Worcester had lived then, and had lived since 1938. This author also went to St John's School - little did he think then that he would one day research this history, find a list of teachers and their addresses and see his own address included. Moreover, Miss Worcester, by this time Mrs Arcaster, after spending some time away from the district, had moved back and was living only a short distance away in Reigate. A reunion was accomplished and Miss Worcester has been of great help with this period of the history.

Miss Panario started in the Girls' School on 1st February and on 2nd February Miss Williams started but by 11.20am had left feeling unwell and also resigned. She probably holds the record for the shortest teaching engagement at St John's ever. Miss Worcester returned the next day to cover the position.

It was in February 1943 when the iron railings were removed from local front gardens to meet national needs, and the Ring and other parts of the common were ploughed as a part of the *Dig For Victory* campaign. The author of this history clearly remembers the railings going but has found only one person who remembers the ploughing of the Ring, a previous pupil whose father had an allotment there. The school sports were held on the lawns until 1947, when the Ring was restored for recreation purposes.

Sporadic air raids continued and, instead of seven men, *'six lady air raid wardens came to examine the children's gas masks'*. The older girls raised £500.0.6 in National Savings for 'Wings for Victory' week, and Empire Day was celebrated in church, as 24th May was very wet. The Boys' School was broken into during July and corrosives from the science cupboard spilt about, damaging record books and 'ruining' the Barnett shield.

Miss Worcester began as a permanent teacher in the Boys' School in August and in October both Miss Panario and Miss Woolley resigned, the former to go to another school, the latter for health reasons. Miss Agate took Miss Woolley's place. Mrs Rouse took time off to be with her husband, home on leave from the RAF, and Miss Worcester found herself in charge of two classes with Mr Bennett's help, and according to him, *'doing quite well'*.

On 3rd December there was no coke in the basement, the boiler was out and the school was cold. Permission to close the school was refused by Dr Bingham but allowed to finish early at 3.45 p.m. What had happened to early closing due to the blackout this year is a bit of a mystery.

In April 1944 an ex-St John's girl, Miss Brewer, became the head of Frenches Road School, taking over from the outgoing holder of that post. Miss Griffin. A native of Reigate, Miss Brewer had attended Reigate County School after St John's and had gone on to be a teacher at Turners Hill School for 3 years. Following training at Goldsmiths College she had spent eleven years at Cromwell Road School and 9 years at South Park School, having left St John's around 1915.

A service was held in Church in April 1944 for a past pupil killed in action, and the children were back in church for Empire Day in May. In June there were some very long air raid alerts that lasted most of the night and into the morning, so few children attended school, which was possibly just as well as Civil Defence personnel had taken it over. On 19th June the nine infants present out of 197 had their dinners served in the air raid shelters. These dinners were provided by the Borough Education Committee and are the first mention in the logs of the dinner service having begun.

Dinners for the Girls' School began on 18th September of 1944, food coming from Reigate at first and not from the central kitchen at Colesmead.

Multiple alerts and the Infants' School being unavailable for use were only compensated for by the weather being so good that lessons could be held outdoors. Even when the school was vacated by the Civil Defence people three alerts a day were not uncommon and children sometimes spent almost all day in the shelters.

On the day of his marriage in July to Dorothy Hood of 18 Gloucester Road, Pilot Officer Raymond Dewey, ex-St John's pupil of 22 Brighton Road heard that he had been awarded the DFC for many successful operations against the enemy.

It was during the summer of 1944 that flying bombs, or Doodlebugs as they were nicknamed, began droning overhead on their way to London. Some fell short, one killing 11 people and injuring many more at Earlswood on 17th June, another killing three workmen at a Merstham depot and blowing in the windows of Merstham School. Some children were cut by flying glass but fortunately a blown-in window frame fell between the rows of children. Yet another damaged Mr Ross' house at Coulsdon severely enough that he had to move out for a while.

Some children were evacuated from St John's because of the flying bomb menace. The Boys' School was used as a registration centre for the evacuees. Children assembled there at 8.30am on 18th July. Some of the St John's evacuees went in groups, some individually, either to the West Country or Wales, with evacuation periods varying from two weeks to six months. The groups went during the summer holidays and had teachers with them. For spending two weeks away with children during holiday time teachers were rewarded with one week's holiday in term time. Infants' teacher, Miss Pickup, plus Boys' School staff members Mr Bennett, Miss Worcester, Mrs Nicholas and Mr Weeds were involved. Miss Worcester and Mrs Nicholas spent two weeks each in South Wales and Mr Weeds went to Bridgend. Mr Bennett spent a month at Cheltenham. Those children evacuated individually and without teachers spent the longest time away.

Maureen Miles

Maureen Miles

Maureen Miles and Joyce Burberry, who are still friends to this day, were evacuated to Wales but not together. Maureen went with her brother on the stipulation that they were not separated but were sent to a house where the lady died after a short while and she was sent elsewhere alone. She spent several months in her room, as she was not allowed out of the house. Maureen still remembers her first day at St John's when she was delighted to find that the plasticine table was just the right height for a child's use; such a change from grown-up furniture at home.

Dudley Waters

Dudley was at St John's from 1937-1946 and also remembers being evacuated with his elder brother to Blaenavon, Monmouth. His time there is summed up in his written reminiscences thus: - '*Not a happy time*'.

He remembers when the Ring was ploughed for allotments, football was played on the Lawns, rugby was played in the area between the school and the laundry, the boys' air raid shelter walls were adorned with paintings, and a boy's father, or other relation, brought a lemon to the school for everyone to see. The laundry also provided entertainment at playtimes when the boys could watch the great wicker baskets being unloaded from vans and pushed down a wooden shute into the bowels of the building. He also distantly remembers a wallaby hunt on the common but does not recall any sightings. This was in 1945 and the local paper's report stated the animal was a kangaroo. Whatever the creature was neither Dudley nor the paper could throw any light on what it was doing there or what became of it.

Miss Worcester took a group of boys to Chessington Zoo. Transport was by bicycle and Dudley went on his brand new 'Federal' Co-op cycle. While there it was stolen. It was not recovered but the Zoo paid Dudley its value, accepting responsibility through his 2d entry ticket, which he had retained.

One sign of the times that Dudley points out is that in those days most boys not only wore short trousers but left school still wearing them!

The End of the War

On 20th February 1945 Miss Ingram, who had resigned as a teacher from the Infants' School in 1932, came to see the children in her capacity as a speech therapist. Perhaps she brought good luck for there were only three more air raid alerts after her visit and, ten weeks later on May the 8th, Victory in Europe (VE) Day was celebrated. The school closed on May 8th and 9th in celebration. The war in the Pacific was to continue for a while but for British civilians and the children of St John's the war was over.

The rest of 1945 had its place in history. Nationally the people understood Britain's foreign policy better than they had before the war and wanted to ensure that what they had been through twice this century already did not happen again. They changed the government, leaving Churchill feeling they were thankless. Internationally, atomic bombs blasted Japan, and Stalin would not budge from declaring his border in Germany. The Atomic Age and the Iron Curtain were upon us.

At a local level the Rev. Ball left the area. Many records show his time at St John's Church ending in 1945 but the Boys' School logs suggest that he left the area on 25th October 1944. He was replaced by the Rev J B Phillips. Empire Day 1945 fell during the Whitsuntide holiday and for the first time in many years was not celebrated, and was not to be marked again. 1945 was the centenary year of the Schools but also seems to have gone unmarked. St John's girls won the inter-schools sports shield for the ninth time.

Log Entry of September 18th 1945 - *'School feeding began. Meals served at St John's Hall'.* So began school dinners for the Boys' School; all children now having access to school dinners if they wanted them.

There are some statistics concerning World War Two and the Borough of Reigate (which did not extend much further towards London than the top of Reigate Hill in those days) that are worth mentioning. During hostilies there were 893 alerts in the Borough. Over 500 bombs fell within its boundaries (not including incendiary devices of which there were over 5000) and 17 flying bombs came down. 50 people were killed and 161 were injured. 115 houses were destroyed and 4000 damaged. 42 of our own unexpended anti-aircraft shells fell back on our own soil, some damaging property, one causing a fatality. Although St John's came through the war undamaged at least 2 other schools did not. As a consequence of the hostilities there was a certain amount of ordnance from various sources left lying around and well into the 1950s police officers were touring schools to impress on children the dangers of touching unidentified metal objects.

The End of the Borough Education Committee

In April 1945 Reigate Borough Education Committee ceased to exist and the school began to be administered by the Surrey County Council. 1845-1903 had seen local managers in charge and 1903-1945 had seen the arrival of the School Board in the shape of the Reigate Borough Council's Education Committee. Now began the era of management that has continued to the present day. The School's new name was 'Reigate St John's County Primary School'. Although the school address was and still is Redhill, the 'Reigate' part was presumably due to the fact that it was located in Reigate Borough.

Chapter Nine
Times of Change, the Post-war Years

The Immediate Post-war Years

Mr Bennett's report for 1946 tells us a great deal about conditions immediately after the war at St John's Boys' School, so much so that it is worth reproducing it here in a slightly edited form.

'It is with considerable pleasure that I present what should have been my 14th annual report but is actually my 8th. It is, however, yet another sign of our return to resettlement and normality, and, we earnestly hope, to peace among nations. One does not hear so much talk today about the total abolition of war but that does not prevent us from expressing that wish, which I feel is in all our hearts.

'This simple function [the meeting at which this report was given] *provides ample evidence of the crowded nature of our school, and its lack of the amenities of a modern building. I regret that I frequently have to refuse likely candidates for admission, for the school continues to maintain its popularity. Whatever its future – and as a school in this present building I fear it is doomed to extinction within the period of the next few years – we shall all endeavour to keep its tradition in all its phases. It is not my province to make known to you what the possible outlook may be, (you have access to the same source of information that I have: namely our efficient local paper, the Surrey Mirror). I am faced – after the summer holiday – with a considerable influx to the extent of a probable roll of nearly 260; this number divided among six teachers (we have only six classrooms) reveals the size of classes we may expect.*

'If you come to see us, and I hope to give you the opportunity on an ordinary school day, you will realise some of the distractions and interruptions we have to contend with. To change classrooms, involved by a limited form of specialisation, produces something in the nature of a small earthquake; and we are faced with a year during which there will be no leavers, as the raising of the school age to 15 is to be implemented next April.

'Educational advancement is slowly taking place. The past two years have seen the introduction of school dinners. More than 140 meals are served in the parish hall, and this number cannot be increased. At present we have a band of helpers as good as any and a waiting list of boys waiting to be included. The provision of school milk is to be extended to all the pupils without charge. How glad we are to return to the delivery of the individual bottle instead of dishing out daily from larger quantities.

93

'We have seen some changes in our staff. Mr Nicholas has been away to improve his already high qualifications as a teacher of Arts and Crafts, and Mrs Nicholas has carried on in her husband's place. Mr Jones was cordially welcomed on his return from military service in the Near East and Palestine. He has not yet told us of all his experiences. Mrs Bonner gave us valuable assistance until his return. Our National Savings Association has become an integral part of almost every school, and ours is well managed by Mr Ross, our senior assistant. Mr Mole is the assistant with the longest service in this school and is responsible for the senior boys. Mr Weeds is in charge of a large dual class. They are all responsible for special subjects and with versatility take older and younger pupils with equal success. Miss Worcester does good work with the small boys; she is in charge of the nature study and takes all the music.

'I must mention the very valuable help we receive from Miss Willett, our school helper. She is a most efficient secretary and to me indispensable. She frequently tells me that she wonders how we managed to do our many tasks before she came. As you walk round the building you will see the need for considerable attention from a builder and decorator. You will notice that our Honours Board, erected on the occasion of our 50th anniversary of the foundation of this building as a separate Boys' School, is nearly full. Recently 56 names were added, being those obtained during the 7 war years. Although one of the leanest years I have known in the field of sport I feel we are on the up-grade. Last week we held our own sports meeting on a reduced scale on the Lawns but look forward to a time in the near future when we can return to a more ambitious programme at the Earlswood Ring as in former years.

'I, in your name, extend a cordial welcome to Mr Dudley Bull, who is headmaster of a well-known school and has had a long association with the school as a manager. We are grateful to him for taking the place of the Chairman of the Managers, the Rev J.B.Phillips, who is now away on a short holiday. I am glad that we have been able to revive the church services that we have had from time to time in the church.

'To those of you who go away empty handed, and who have seen others get prizes, I would say, in the words of that famous quotation,

> And when the master scorer comes
> To write against your name.
> He'll write not that you lost or won,
> But how you played the game.'

Much of the report is self-explanatory. Miss Willett had began only that year as a clerical assistant in the Boys' School and Mrs Lee had begun in a similar post in the Infants' School, the first mention of these posts. Mr Jones had returned from Military service on 4th February 1946 to teaching at St John's. Ernest Bevan had announced that 750,000 servicemen would be out of uniform that year but was aware of mistakes made about the order of demobilisating people at the end of the previous war. Personnel were therefore classified A or B, the latter being craftsmen or tradesmen who would be released first. They would have to return to their old trades and not take up new ones.

Surprisingly there were still 46,000 evacuated children away from their homes in 1946. Nevertheless things would soon return to normal and Mr Bennett would be able to continue writing his usual reports. No doubt the Headmistress of the Girls' School was very pleased to be able to

St John's girls on the first post-war school trip to London in 1945.
Courtesy Alan Horwood

write ordinary things again in her reports, such as that the radio in the Girls' School was being used to listen to the Radio Doctor, and that Mr Newell came about the proposed safety barrier - presumably at the Pendleton Road end of the slope. Something not quite so normal was that there was a church service for Brian King, aged 12; no other information about this is available.

On 10th December an advisor came about the school garden project. This refers to the creation of a garden in the area where the pond is now and resulted in the boys, under the direction and guidance of the appropriately named Mr Weeds, forming the terrace and building the concrete retaining walls we see there now. Long gone flowerbeds were also created.

1947 began with the worst winter for many years. It lasted into March 1948 and reduced attendance considerably. It was not conducive to cheering up a nation where post-war austerity and travel restrictions were dominant features. To make matters worse there were boiler problems in the lower school in January and the boys wore overcoats in class. The boiler burst in the upper building in the middle of October and was not mended until the middle of November. Paraffin heaters were brought into some classes but class 4 and the babies had to take turns in class 4 where the canteen hotplate gave some heat. This was the classroom at the west end of the upper building. The reason for the hotplate was that children ate their dinners in the hall. The partition was pushed back and the food served from that class. Classes 2 and 3 were taught in the staff room where there was a gas fire. This is now the Head's office.

A major change to the school occurred in 1947 when the senior boys and girls, those aged 12-15 were transferred to secondary schools and the Boys' and Girls' Schools began to cater for juniors drawn from outlying districts, presumably meaning further away than other schools in Redhill and Reigate that they had already been coming from. Those from the two major contributory schools started at different ages, St John's Infants' at 7+ and those from Earlswood at 8+, which created some problems. Hooley School became a secondary school. Another change was that the Management Committee merged with the Management Committee of Earlswood County Secondary and County Primary Schools in 1949. The reason for this is unknown; perhaps School Managers were hard to come by. The changes probably reflected the policies of the County Council, the new Local Education Authority since 1945.

The school concert took place at the Central Hall again with 61 boys taking part. On 23rd July the school song was sung in school, and this is the last mention, perhaps the last rendering, of it. Two days later Mr Mole went into hospital.

The School on the Common

On return to school the staff and classes in the Boys' School were arranged: -

Form 1	Std 4+	Mr Jones	33
Form 2	Std 3A	Mr Mole	32
Form 3	Std 3B	Mr Ross	33
Form 4	Std 2A	Mr Weeds	29
Form 5	Std 2B	Mr Miller	36
Form 6	Std 1	Miss Worcester	35

On 8th September Mr Mole came to school to report himself unfit for duty. On the 12th he was back in hospital and was not expected to return. He died the following April. Two old pupils made a prayer desk in memory of Mr Mole, a family present that was dedicated by the vicar at the Boys' School in January 1949.

School was closed for the wedding of Princess Elizabeth on 19th November 1947. The Princess needed to get extra ration coupons for her dress material. Another Royal occasion, the silver wedding of the King and Queen, closed the school for a half day on 26th April 1948. On May 6th Empire Day was recorded by a special mention at assembly and the whole school listened to a special twenty-minute broadcast about the Empire at 11am. In November the Boys' School was re-organised with boys coming in from county schools. In December a break-in netted over £11 dinner money from Mr Bennett's desk.

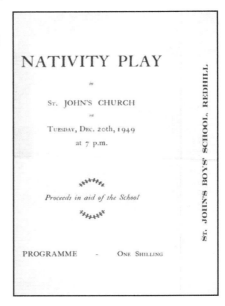

The decade ended without the optimism expressed in Mr Bennett's 1946 report regarding an improvement in sporting success coming to fruition, although within a couple of years this would improve.

A nativity play was performed in front of parents, starting a tradition of such seasonal events that lasted some years, the creative force behind those up to 1950 being Miss Worcester. The programmes here are from 1949 and 1950 and the accompanying picture shows the cast from one of the plays in the 1940s. Picture courtesy Maureen Miles, programmes courtesy Mrs Arcaster (Miss Worcester)

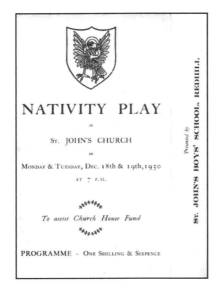

Moore Recollections

Alan Moore

My mother left me in the playground on my first day at St John's School in a state of total distress - mine not hers - and, with other similarly distraught infants, I was part of a little wailing row on a bench outside the door through which more adventurous first day infants had already passed. Through it I too duly passed but few memories of my time in the Infants' School are as vivid as those first ten minutes or so.

Alan Moore

In the 'Big Boys' as the Boys' School was known, I remember that there was a memorial church service for Mr Mole, with the whole Boys' School crocodiling down the slope, across the road, through the gate, up the long entrance way and into the church on a warm and sunny day. All except me, that was. I was stopped from entering the church by a master because I did not have a jacket on. I had to return to the school and spend most of the afternoon here alone. It was a difficult thing for me to understand. My jacket - I had only one - was reserved for autumn and winter. What had God got against shirtsleeves?

Other memories include gardening sessions with Mr Weeds and taking silver bottle tops saved by the school to the old East Surrey Hospital for money to be raised through recycling. There was also a play in which my grand entrance was marked by tripping on the top step up to the stage and sprawling full length and flat on my face in front of the audience of parents and older children. The remainder of my performance in that play was marked by referring to the object that sat stage centre for the whole play, and was supposed to be magic <u>stone</u>, as a *stove*. The script I had learnt was hand written and the N looked like a V.

Corporal punishment in the Boy's School was administered exclusively by the Headteacher; there was a cane on the wall of his office. My memory is crystal clear on that, as is the memory of many other boys who have been in Mr Bennett's office a few times when it was no longer on the wall but in his hand. Once that point in an interview with the Head had been reached the smaller of the people present knew it was going to be used and it was going to hurt - a lot.

Regardless of the offence, the only worthwhile strategy for the pupil was that of saving face during the administration of the punishment. This was achieved by firmly holding out each hand in turn for the requisite number of strokes, usually three on each, while fixing the Head firmly and unblinkingly in the eye and showing no emotion. This was actually quite difficult because *his* eye was on your outstretched hand. Miss Willett's desk was in Mr Bennett's office; sometimes you could fix her in the eye instead.

When all six strokes had been administered the Head would dismiss the subject of his corrective efforts. Most boys would walk steadily to the door, open it, step outside, close the door firmly, carefully check that no one else was around and then, thrusting throbbing fingers under opposite armpits, hop about muttering until either someone came along or the pain subsided sufficiently for normal progress to be made back to class. There, entrance would be made and seat taken as though the trip to the head's office had been simply to receive congratulations with regard to how well one's studies were progressing.

Corporal punishment, as we all know, is now not carried out in schools. I have been asked several times during the compilation of this history if it did him any harm. The answer is no. Did it do any good? Boys certainly didn't go home and tell their parents about it because more displeasure - all directed at them - would have been incurred, and therein lies the difference between then and now.

The beams in the lower building hall, now the gymnasium and dining hall but once divided into classrooms, were exposed then, and when the teacher was out of the room pens could be thrown up to stick in them. The beams had hundreds of pens stuck in them. The handles fell out of some leaving just the nibs there. It was a caning offence and the imaginative part was explain to the teacher on his return why you had nothing to write with now yet you did before he went out - quite a challenge.

I also remember tobogganing down the hill from the Top Common, although I had a plank of wood instead of a toboggan. It worked well, sliding down the hill fast enough to be exhilarating; controllable to the point of being death defying (which meant there was no control whatsoever), and made me want to lug it all the way back to the top to do it again. The square-cut leading edge sprayed up so much snow that it was impossible to see where I was going but it was great fun.

Old pictures of the common show it quite bare of vegetation. When I was at St John's there was much more growth, such as the gorse, the seeds pods of which cracked open and sounded like gunfire on very hot summer days. As I got older I walked back and forth over the common to school, taking this path and that and getting to know it well. That was when Ted Gould was the common keeper and looked after it in-between chasing boys like me off it. The body responsible for the maintenance of the common, the Common Conservators, was dissolved in 1945 and the common has since reverted somewhat more to the wild, with even more growth.

My memories of the war include encountering a column of tanks while on my way to school one day. It came up Mill Street and continued down Whitepost Hill. The drivers' heads were sticking out of the front of the tanks. Some smiled at me and I probably just stared blankly back. The column went to Reigate and I went to St John's, noting that the road surface after their passing was not quite as it was before. I remember on several occasions hearing gunfire from the sky and seeing vapour trails. I remember lying in bed and hearing bombers go over at night (before we got the Anderson shelter and I had to sleep in the basement). There were so many aircraft that the roar of their engines used to go in and out of synchronisation and produce that rhythmic beat heard in old war films.

And I remember the doodlebug. I was walking towards St John's School and had just reached the peak of the Top Common before the descent to the school when it came over. It was directly overhead when the engine cut out. I had heard that when this happened the doodlebug went into a spiralling dive and exploded directly below where its fuel had run out. This was obviously the end of me. I was still rooted to the spot when I realised that it wasn't spiralling at all but going into a gentle but perfectly straight dive. It exploded a couple of miles away somewhere near Merstham (it wasn't the one that damaged Merstham School) and I watched it all the way.

I have written about evacuation in this history but all I know about it I have found out from others or from research. I had no personal experience of it, remaining at home throughout the war. I have asked my mother if she was ever approached about my removal elsewhere and she says she never was. What the qualifying criteria were I do not know.

Ex-Teacher Mrs Barratt 1937-1947

Where the library now is was once a classroom designated Green Class. This was Mrs Barratt's classroom. It had a fireplace and once was the place from where the school bell was rung by a rope that led into the bell tower. Access was from the infants' hall. Access from the girls' hall to the infants' hall was via a corridor through what is now the boys' toilets.

Mrs Barratt remembers Head Mistress Miss Towell as being aloof and strict and Miss White as being friendly and up and coming. She doesn't remember the war as having too great an effect on school life - she wasn't affected by the sharing of the premises with other schools, for example - but she did go away for two weeks to Bridgend with some of the evacuated children when the flying bombs started coming over. She also remembers telling the children what a wonderful day VE day was when it came.

It was Mrs Barratt who especially remembered one of her pupils, a New Zealand girl named Fleur Adcock, the name sticking in her mind, and she was later to hear her on the radio. In 2000 Fleur Adcock OBE was contacted and visited St John's. More about that later.

The 1950s

The replacement of the slate by ink and as a writing medium was a significant step forward. Just as significant, perhaps, was the advent of the ball pen, or biro, that began to replace ink in the school logs at the very end of 1949 and became fairly common in 1950.

A complaint in February 1950 about the school dinners resulted in an official from the Education Department coming to sample them. News of his visit was obviously received beforehand by the kitchens for he and everyone else tasted the best dinner the school had enjoyed for a long time.

Susan Hayward (presumably not THE Susan Hayward) was May Queen in 1950. 28th July was Head Mistress Mrs Faulkner's last day as head of the Infants' School. She had been Head Mistress for almost 17 years, having started in September 1933. On 1st September 1950 Miss J D M Kirkham took her place. Miss Faulkner lived in

Mr Bennett and Mr Jones with the 1950-51 football team. The team, from left to right, is:-
front seated - David Branch, Kenny Bailey. Second row - Alan Love, Tony Tailor, Tiddler Powell (Capt), David Jones, Colin Pierpoint.
Back row - with flag Niel Kearns (probably the linesman) Kenny Carter, Goalkeeper Allsop?, David or Nigel Bevan and John Button.
Picture and names courtesy of John Button

Reigate and died only about three years before the writing of this history was begun.

The floors of the school were 'oiled' in 1952, ending the need for scrubbing that must have been carried out for years. Everyone was presumably happy about this except perhaps Mrs Purpoint, the lady who carried out the scrubbing, and whose services were no longer required. The log recording this, '*The services of Mrs Purpoint, scrubber, will no longer be required*' might be slightly rephrased today. Those who attended the school in the nineteen-twenties remember getting splinters in their backsides from sitting on the floor, and that the building always had the musty, dusty smell that comes from untreated wood floors.

A long period of silence about sporting achievements ended with the Boys' School log entry, '*The boys of the football team, with Mr Jones, went to Horley to receive the Borough Junior Schools Football cup which they have won*'. This was followed in July with, '*Junior Borough Sports; Boys won Challenge Cup*', and in July 1952 with, '*We retained Boys' Championship Trophy*'.

In 1951 Mrs Cross was made temporary Deputy Head of the Infants' School, the first time the post had existed. When she left in 1952 Mrs Housman took over. The criterion for the post was the presence of more than 200 infant children. Miss Worcester and Mr Weeds both left St John's Boys' School in 1951.

1952 started with Winston Churchill once again Prime Minister. February 6th, 1952 saw the death of King George VI; some of the children listened to the proclamation of Queen Elizabeth II on the radio two days later. Children also gave a Coronation display of dancing miming and figure marching in front of governors and parents to celebrate the forthcoming coronation of Queen Elizabeth on 2nd June. They took part in Coronation festivities at the Ring and went to the Odeon cinema in Redhill on 16th June with the rest of the school to the see the film *A Queen is Crowned*. In the same month of June the school received a visit from old boy Sydney Cooper, who had left in 1913 and was making a return visit to this country from Australia.

On the subject of films, 1952 was the year of *Singing in the Rain* with Gene Kelly. Charlie

May Day 1951. The girl and boy on the far left are identified by the contributor of this picture as Jean Whitmore and Graham Huish respectively.

Chaplin made *Limelight,* and Marilyn Monroe burst upon the scene in *Niagara*.

The infant children started using the basement as a canteen, specially fitted out for the purpose, when they returned from their Easter holidays in 1953. Some of the teachers went on courses concerned with intelligence testing of the children and tests were carried out in the school (roots of baseline testing?).

At the end of the summer term Mr Bennett recorded the following log entry: - '*Prizegiving: I was presented with a cheque and the accompanying letter: - This cheque, the gift of the managers, staff, boys (and some old boys) is presented to Mr R.G.Bennett to mark their sincere appreciation of his 21 years service as Headmaster of St John's Boys' School. It is offered with gratitude and affection and the sincere wish that he may enjoy a well-earned and happy retirement.*'

Another era was at an end, following on from so many other eras highlighted in this history. Each and every one is stamped by the personality and achievements of the people who defined them, and in this case by another Head who had seen the Boys' School through a World War, as had Mr Jinks before him. Mr Bennett's retirement was to last for under six years, his funeral in December 1958 being attended, among others, by Mr Jones and Miss Willett.

Mr Wise and Mr Booth left St John's at the same time as Mr Bennett. In September 1953 Mr Francis George Boddington took temporary charge of the Boys' School and on 9th April 1954 Miss White retired from the Headship of the Girls' School.

This was almost the beginning of another era, for on 2nd October 1953 it is recorded that, '*A service of dedication was held this afternoon at the site of the new school in Sandcross Lane. The foundation stone was unveiled by the Mayor of Reigate, Alderman H.Daniels J.P., and the building dedicated by the Lord Bishop of Kingston.*' Exactly one month later a surveyor called at the old school, '*in connection with the valuation of the school premises prior to the sale to the authorities.*' St John's Boys' School was about to leave the site it had occupied since October 1884 and move to new premises, the old building being sold by the church to the Local Education Authority. Mr Bennett returned to present the prizes at the school sports on 15th July 1954. Eight days later a Boys' School log entry read, '*The school closes today for the summer holiday. After 70 years in the present building will re-open after the holiday as St John's C of E Primary Mixed School, Sandcross Lane, Reigate.*'

Although this history is about our site and the St John's School that today retains that name whilst the Sandcross Lane School does not, the logbook recording these events was taken to the new Sandcross Lane building, so we take a brief look at the logs of the new school in order to glean any information that might be of use.

Two things are of immediate interest. The first is about the opening of the new school at Sandcross Lane. On 31st August the logbook starts recording events there, including the fact that the nominal roll was 308 in seven classes of 44 maximum accommodation each. On 6th October the Rev J.B.Phillips conducted the Harvest Festival Service, more or less confirming that 'our' school was no longer a church school, that function being transferred to the new premises. And he also conducted the official opening service on 3rd November 1954, the school being closed for the event (almost a contradiction in terms).

The second is the recorded death on 3rd December 1954 of Miss Ethel Ramsay aged 91. Members of the Ramsay family had been associated with the school since at least 1886, and Miss Ethel Ramsay almost all of her life, and a revealing log entry is contained in the logbook for the year of her death.

'In March 1949, when the school was in the old building, urgently needed repairs brought a financial crisis. When the managers reluctantly decided that the school must be handed over to the County Authority, and arrangements were in hand for this to be done, Miss Ramsay offered a personal gift of £300 to retain St John's as a church school. Although the gift was anonymous, and the name of the donor known only to the necessary few, it is right that it should now be recorded here. Miss Ramsay was 91 and this school is but one body that owes much to her lifetime of devoted Christian service.'

The old school was now in the hands of the education authorities but the new was not, and this log entry reveals information not revealed by the 1949 logs, so reading on through the transfer was very worthwhile. St John's School at Sandcross Lane was eventually to separate entirely and be renamed St Luke's as a closer reflection of its new location at South Park. The direct link between the Church old School on the Common had ended in 1954; this was the end of the direct link between St John's Church and any St John's School. Of course, 150 years and more of history and the proximity of St John's Church and School mean that they still retain considerable ties.

We now return to 1954 with continuing events at the old location, now in use by the new *County Boys', Girls' and Infants' Schools*, and where, on 28th April 1954, Mr Shaw, the School Welfare Officer, talked to the top three classes about the local area as he and his family had known it for more than 100 years. He was part of the family after which Shaws Corner was named. The Head Mistress of the Girls' School attended the laying of the foundation stone for St Bede's School on 1st October.

School visits to places of interest in London, including a boat trip on the Thames, still took place from time to time throughout the 1950s. There were also local visits, one of which the laundry next to the school hosted. On 13th March 1955 a party of Form III girls visited the Refuse Disposal Works. Girls went to farms to see milk production and haymaking and in 1957 visited the Ancient House Bookshop in Reigate to look at and choose books for the school. A number of field study trips were made to Box Hill. In July Miss Wright, who had taught at St John's Girls' School in 1915-16 came to talk about the differences between then and the current time. Teachers looked back in the logbooks and found entries referring to her at that time.

From the end of WW2 the number of mentions of events that at one time had closed the school for all or half a day, or finished work earlier in the afternoon, had further reduced. There was no more mention of circuses, although no doubt they still visited, or of Sunday School or Band of Hope excursions to the coast, weekday fetes, flower shows and so on. Ascension Day was a day of closure but many of the children and staff would attend services at St John's Church, and one visit to London involved at least the whole of the Girls' School, effectively being a closure although education continued off-site. There were closures for some royal events, of course, but even these happened less often. Inter-school sporting events and the annual school leavers excursion to places of educational interest were perhaps by now the major single pauses in the year, acting a little like the commas in this text. For this reason it was perhaps an almost major occasion when the school closed for the day on 16th December 1956 to celebrate the winning of the Primary Schools Swimming Cup.

In the summer of 1957 a Girls' School log entry reads, *'A member of the police force spoke to the girls about the dangers of touching any explosives they might find lying about.'* one of the references to leftover wartime ordnance made earlier in this history. Two years later the exercise was repeated, but this time the entry refers to *'unfamiliar metal objects'.* The war had finished fourteen years earlier.

This was the era of royal blue knickers for girls during PE lessons, and the purchase of new PE equipment was the object of a sale organised by girls leaving at the end of the 1958 summer term. Intruders damaged PE equipment in October but whether it was the same equipment the money had been raised for is unknown. Six months later PE boxes were accidentally smashed by the dinner van. Other equipment mentioned in logs around this time was the new locker desks, the arrival of the final consignment of which heralded the departure of the last of the old desks. Today desks have been replaced by tables and chairs but over the years there must have been a number of different models, starting from the tiered galleries of the 1850s and 60s, through the four-seater 'Osborne Reversible' of the later part of the previous century. It would be interesting to see examples of each stood together for comparison.

The inspector's report for 1958/9 refers to the *'rather antiquated basins'* in the girls' cloakroom as *'now supplied with hot water'.* If this can be taken as meaning that hot water was a recent provision – and this same year the paper towels were replaced by Towelmasters – then it is a small surprise that only cold had hitherto been available and perhaps, with a number of other aspects of progress since then, shows how far some of the comforts we now take for granted have come.

The report also notes that several of the rooms had, *'interesting displays of pictures and materials; books chosen with care and discrimination and attractively displayed.'* This history has not mentioned pictures or any other brightening of the school since the 1870-1903 period, mainly because the logs have been silent on the subject, but it can be safely assumed that the children in all departments were gradually provided with, and contributed to, visual enhancement that both stimulated them and congratulated them on their achievements, greatly relieving what must have been a much more austere presentation of the premises in the previous century.

At the beginning of 1958 Infants' Head Miss Kirkham left to take up the headship of an infants' school at Morden and her place was taken by Mrs Tharp. She was to see out a decade, marked in its last year by the marriage of Princess Margaret, that had seen a certain amount of change but was still a period when blackboards needed to be re-blacked regularly, 'party-line' telephones were common and diphtheria immunisation was still given.

About Alan Wilkinson

Ex-St John's pupil Alan is a full-time professional writer and historian. He dropped out of formal education at 19 but returned in his late 30s to take a First in American Studies at Hull (& New Mexico), and an M.A. in Creative Writing at UEA. Since 1993 writing has been his sole source of income. His broadcast media work has mainly been in writing voice-overs for documentaries such as: *Holiday Reps, Superstore, Zoo Keepers, Life of Grime, War and Piste* and *Surviving the Iron Age, Love Is Not Enough* (the series on adoption), and the children's series *Trading Places*; plus ITV's *Trauma Team.* He is now working on the final series of the ever-popular *Vets In Practice.* Ventures into drama include half a dozen episodes of *Emmerdale .* He has lived in and written about New Mexico and travelled widely on the Great Plains. In 1994 he borrowed a bicycle in Lincoln, Nebraska and cycled 630 miles across the state in a September heatwave. He has also crossed the Plains from south to north, following the 100th Meridian from the Mexican border to the Canadian line. He has written travel pieces for a number of national newspapers and magazines, is involved in biographical writing, and works with private clients on autobiographical or family history projects. Alan has also worked on two collections of love-letters telling the story of an

Alan Wilkinson

Edwardian courtship conducted from the trenches of WWI. For fifteen years or more he taught at University level and has set up and run several writing workshops in Adult and Continuing Education. Also he has been a correspondence tutor for the Open College of the Arts, and serves as Assessment Officer for their writing courses.

In His Own Words - Alan Wilkinson's Reminiscences

I started at St John's school on a Thursday in the spring of 1956. I had just moved house from Merstham to Meadvale. My older brother Anthony, three years above me, started on the Wednesday: my father wasn't very organised. I remember going for an interview with Mr Mitchell in his office at the front of the school. He had some sort of reptile in a glass jar on his desk and he asked me what it was. I thought it might be a lizard, but no - it was a newt. Being only six, I should have gone into the Infants, but apparently there was no room there, so I went into the youngest class to complete the school year and stayed down the following September, by which time I was seven.

Our teacher in the first year was Mr Ross, a nice man in his silver-haired sixties who read us John Buchan stories - Prester John and so on. We liked him. He also read us stories from *The Jungle Book*, I remember. However, that first term I was in a flat spin, because they were all using 'real writing' - ie, cursive - and I'd never been taught that. So I sat there and laboriously copied what he wrote on the board - "Thursday 23rd April, 1956". I even copied the little knot he scratched at the start of his 'T' to get his dry chalk moving on the squeaky board.

The class was also into some very complicated type of arithmetic, such as I'd never met before. I thought and thought and thought and it slowly dawned on me that they were doubling everything: it was multiplication. So I doubled everything in my exercise book... only to come to grief when they moved on to multiplying by three. Nobody ever asked me whether I was familiar with these things. I was just left to get on with it.

I don't remember much about my first full year except that Mr Ross retired at the end of it (I think) and that what seemed like a few months later Mr Mitchell announced in assembly that he had died.

For Year Two we went with Mr Pratt, a red-haired man who lived in Frenches Road. Our classroom was one of three in a row that were separated by sliding glazed doors and made up the assembly hall. We liked Mr Pratt, and I suppose he must have quite liked us as a class, because we kept him for the next three years. I remember us cheering when he announced the fact that he would be staying with us into Year Three.

There was a music teacher, Mr Lofts, who played the piano for assembly. He suddenly became ill, went absent, and died. He was replaced at very short notice by a Mr Nevvy - I think that was his name. He was an oddity in that he didn't play the piano, so our hymns at morning assembly were sung to the accompaniment of his violin.

In assembly we always - or often - had a piece of classical music played on the gramophone. One of our favourites was the *William Tell* Overture, which of course was the signature tune to our favourite Saturday morning tv show, *The Lone Ranger*. The music teacher once told us that if anyone ever dared call it "the Lone Ranger music" they'd be in big trouble. Some months later it came around again, and the question was asked: what's this called? It was a boy who gloried in the name of Howard Goodenough who thrust his hand up and said "The Lone Ranger". I think he got a wallop round the side of his head, amid much merriment.

Playtime was interesting. After Year Two, I think, we were allowed outside the playground - just about anywhere, so long as we could hear the whistle. We played marbles up against the outside of the playground wall, watched the vans coming and going at the Snowflake Laundry (I think it was called that), and chatted to the boiler-man-and-caretaker, who showed us magic tricks; or we gathered beech mast beneath the giant tree under which the staff parked their cars - and got told off for munching it in class later. It must have been late 1959 or early 1960 when one of the teachers showed up in a flashy new Triumph Herald - much to the delight of us boys. In the summer we picked up sycamore seeds off the ground, peeled the base open and stuck the gluey insides to our noses. Just outside the playground gate was a concrete monolith of some sort - perhaps a remnant of an air-raid shelter - which we used to rush to 'occupy' at the start of playtime, spending the next half hour or so defending it against wave after wave of invaders.

We also had epic games of cricket, using a sycamore tree over by the laundry as a wicket. Occasionally Mr Mitchell would come out and roll up his sleeves and the boys would beg him to take the bat. He'd push his shirt-cuffs back, shove his elastic arm-bands further up his arm, and take strike. He couldn't half hit the ball, and he liked to whack it as high as he could and challenge us to catch it. He was full of surprises. One day, looking up at the laundry chimney, he offered a prize to whoever could guess its height. We never heard any more of it, unfortunately. He was like that: throwing out surprise challenges when he felt like it. One time he gave us till Monday morning to write a short essay explaining why square wheels wouldn't work. We all knew it was "blinking obvious", but nobody had the faintest idea how to express it. I don't think Mr Mitchell ever took on a challenge he couldn't be pretty sure of winning.

Outside on the margins of the common we ran relay races up and down the gravelled lane that led up to some picturesque old cottages, and we raced our Dinky toys in little rabbit-runs that scarred the grassy slopes. I remember playing a game whereby pairs of boys dragged us on our backs down the grassy slope. The time I did it I landed on some glass and had to make the short journey to the County Hospital to have my first ever stitch.

When we played in the playground, I remember, we used to get fantastically hot: it was all tarmac, surrounded on three sides by buildings and it faced south. Having to stand still, in lines, and wait to be called to march inside at the end of the lunch-break could be absolute agony. As soon as we got past the toilets and into the cloakroom we'd plunge our heads in the wash-basins and pour cold water over our hair, and drink as much as we could to last us through the next lesson.

Lunchtimes we formed into crocodiles and marched past the church, along Pendleton Road and across the A23 to a sort of shed, like a scout hut, that stood - and I think still stands - at a junction right beside the Brighton Road. In the summer we were walked in long lines down to Redhill for our swimming-lessons. Otherwise, there was PE, which took place in the playground. We wore coloured sashes according to our house - Scott, Hunt, Fleming or Elgar - and played things like tunnel-ball. The formal games periods would frequently involve a walk down the The Ring, not far from Earlswood Lakes, for cricket or football; and in summer we had some sort of school sports day at a delightful venue, The Lawns, on the Top Common: cool velvety grass shaded by tall trees. I well remember the slow bicycle race, sack race and egg-and-spoon race, played with a tennis ball. Once a year - well, I can remember it happening at least twice in my four years - we all trooped down town for the district school sports competition which took place in the old Memorial Sports Ground on the same hallowed turf where Redhill FC of the Athenian League strutted their stuff.

I remember quite a few of my contemporaries. I've barely clapped eyes on any of them in the 32 years since I left. I went straight to boarding school in September 1960, from there to London, and in 1973 to Yorkshire, where I still live. Here is a list of names I recall, most of whom would have spent the same three years as I did in Mr Pratt's class.

Ian Sherlock; Christopher Cornish (who was Head Boy in Year Four); David Brand (Deputy Head Boy); 'Fatty' Freeman; Peter Unwin; David Mayne (whom Mr Mitchell always referred to as 'Might and Mayne'); Peter Avis (who passed his 11+); Steven Jacobs; Hilliard Simmonds; John Fredersdorff (who almost passed his 11+ and went for interview, result unknown); Tom Brown. Somebody called Waller - possibly John and somebody called Warren - possible David (one of these two had a mother who came in as a supply teacher when Mr Ross was ill once); Steven Barnard (who went into the Navy as a cadet); Ian Hamilton (who lived next to me in Arbutus Close) Peter Easton; Howard Goodenough; Tony Tullet; Geoffrey Bellinger; ...somebody Jordan; Barry Hutton (who lived in one of the beautiful little houses beside the school and opposite the church); Terry Ede; a couple of Bakers; Philip Dalton (also of Arbutus Close); Dumbrill; Balcombe.

Chapter Ten
Reorganisation in the 1960s and 1970s

Into the 1960s

It was the wish of the Queen that schools should take a holiday upon the occasion of the wedding of Princess Margaret to Mr Anthony Armstrong-Jones on 6th May 1960. Later that summer the girls won the Reigate Girls' Schools Rounders Cup, and in the autumn Woodhatch Secondary School (now the Reigate School) opened. By this time the dreaded diphtheria was a disease rarely - if ever - mentioned in log entries, although immunisation was still offered and taken up by a good number of children. The names used for the four 1930s houses of the Girls' School, Johnson, Nightingale, Eliot and Anderson, had fallen into disuse and in 1961 were replaced by Kings, Pendleton and two unrecorded others. In the Boys' School the Houses at this time were Hunt, Scott, Fleming and Elgar.

'While having a games lesson on Redhill Common, Form 1 was surprised to observe a deer running down the slope and into the trees. This seems sufficiently unusual an occurrence to merit recording', reads a 1962 log entry. From 1943-1950 the compiler of this history walked many times over the common to and from school from Upper Bridge Road and played on it frequently. He saw red squirrels now and then but never a deer. One of the reasons was no doubt that the Common Conservators maintained the common with a staff of men who kept grass cut and much other growth down. Now that much the common is reverting to woodland and is far less open, deer are quite common, as can be verified by Mrs Carpenter, who lives on its edge and has difficulty keeping them out of her garden. Perhaps this early deer was an ancestor of the current herd.

An evening meeting of parents, pupils, past pupils, staff and friends of all three parts of the school was held in the Girls' School on 12th June 1962 when three speakers came to talk about the History of St John's School. Mr Surman of the Educational Research Association spoke on the history of Surrey education; Mrs MacNeil, Headmistress, spoke on the building of St John's School in 1845, and Mr Shaw, ex-Welfare Officer, spoke on Redhill of old. On 15th November 1962 the Surrey Travelling Library Service brought 100 books and borrowing by children for home reading was begun.

Numbers on role fell to 118 in the Girls' School from a high of over 200 in 1951. Although the role of Deputy Head had been dependent at that time on numbers remaining over 200 the post still remained filled as the staff number dropped from five-and-a-half to three in early 1963, with no girls coming to

The rabbit goes to school. Gary Green, left, taking his rabbit to St John's School with the help of his friend, David Maynard, in March 1964. Picture courtesy Gary Green

The School on the Common

St John's from Earlswood School. This was the year when the Borough of Reigate was 100 years old (still 18 years younger than St John's School, of course), and 'Education Fortnight', May 20th - 31st, was a part of the celebration during which the inter-school sports and various demonstrations and open days were held.

An overnight electrical fire in the Boys' School in March 1964 burnt itself out without spreading to other parts of the building. This seems to be very fortunate considering that the school was being redecorated at the time and paint, which is very flammable and could have contributed to a much bigger fire, was stored there.

In March 1963, the news had first been broken of the proposed merger of the Boys' and Girls' Schools under a single Head. Mr Mitchell retired as Head of the Boys' School at the end of the Spring term of 1964, and at the start of the Autumn term this major event in the history of the schools occurred. The school re-opened in its new form as St John's County Junior School, with the Boys' and Girls' departments amalgamated. On role were 194 children, 105 boys and 89 girls, and five mixed classes were formed plus 4A boys and 4A girls in which the oldest children were taught. Both buildings were in use with two classes, a library reading room and a dining hall (with a wash-up kitchen only) in the lower building. In the upper building were five classes, a library reading room and the assembly hall. Some structural alterations were being made to link the two playgrounds via a gate, provide a path from the top of the slope into the lower garden and modify the toilets. This was the first step to the beginning of the school as it is organised today, with the head of the Girls' School, Mrs MacNeil, taking over the two departments, with the Infants' School remaining separate under its own Head, Mrs Tharp (see also appendix 1).

A weekend visit to Belgium and Holland by 40 of the oldest boys and girls in company of Mrs MacNeil and five other adults was labelled a success. It was also one of the most ambitious outings ever. The weather was good and the children had the opportunity to see and learn a great deal. Shortly after this event the school was broken into and just over £2 intended for staff leaving presents stolen. On a happier note, the following month the girls won the 'small schools' athletics cup and a new reason to close the school was found - the 750th anniversary of the signing of the Magna Carta on 16th July. Another era at St John's ended with the leaving of Mrs MacNeil on 23rd July to take up the headship of a school at Sutton.

In October a television was installed in the lower building, possibly a first for this medium at St John's. It is interesting to note that the logs still refer to the lower building as the Boys' School and the upper building as the Girls' School. School re-opened on 10th January 1966 with Mr Bowden as the new Head. Eight days later the log entries in the book in use since 1924 cease with 49 pages left to go. So far this history has enjoyed the luxury of being compiled from the three separate log books of the Girls', Boys' and Infants' Schools; from now on there is only the one record of events.

An extension of the infants' cloakroom was finished in June 1967. 1968 was remarkable for being very unremarkable - we suffer already from the lack of multiple logbooks and the extra information they supplied.

In March 1969 there was another break-in when dinner money and two stop watches were stolen. The Infants' School was again experiencing a shortage of space in which to house 40 children who were on the waiting list. The problem was partially solved by the opening on the 28th April 1969 of a new classroom in the playground in which 20 of the children were taught in the mornings and the other 20 in the afternoons. In the near future a new scheme of First and Middle Schools was to commence and it was in the same April that the Infants' Head, Mrs Tharp, began a one day a week, 10 week course at Glyn House in preparation for this event.

School visits continued, some to local places of interest, such as Chessington Zoo, and Outwood Windmill, others further afield to Guildford Cathedral, London museums and other attractions such as Regents Park Canal. The School Sports were still held annually, although they had ceased to be at the Ring and were held on the lawns on Redhill Common. School still closed on Ascension Day and Dorking Book Fair Day, and occasionally when the boiler broke down when it was most needed to function. Students and specialists alike came to observe work in the school and managers new and established visited as they always had. Teachers came and went and were also sick, as were the children, but happily not from the old complaints that not only used to regularly close the school but sometimes took lives too. In these years the worst general cause of absence seems to have been the flu. Harvest festivals continued to benefit those in the community most in need, including elderly people in St Anne's, Redhill, a building that then dominated the town but which was to be demolished in 1976.

Before leaving the 1960s we can get more information from the reminiscences of ex-teacher John Beales 1956-1962.

The Reminiscences of ex-teacher John Beales 1956-1962

I was appointed to the staff of St John's Boys' School in the summer of 1956. It was my first teaching job after leaving training college. I was interviewed by the Head, Mr Mitchell, the Rev. S G Dyer of St John's Church, who was chairman of governors, and various other governors who I recall said nothing at all. Although I had applied directly to the school instead of the SCC at Kingston, as I should have done, everyone was very pleasant about it and, as I was the only applicant they had for the vacancy, I got the job and started on September 4th at a salary of £450 per annum.

My first class was in the middle room of the main part of the building where there were three classrooms separated from each other by walls of timber and glass. The lower part of each wall was hinged in sections and could be folded back if required. They were not soundproof so teaching in them involved disturbing the other classes to an extent. One got used to it after a time but if the class either side of the centre was ill-disciplined then the class in the centre was disturbed, and if the centre class was noisy it disturbed the classes on either side.

Each of these classes communicated with each other by means of a door in the partition, and a door led from the centre room into the area known as the lobby. During the course of my time there a door leading out through the north wall was made in the centre classroom. On the south

Mr Beales' Plan of the Boys' School in 1956

side of the building were two other classes. These were self-contained with exits to cloakrooms and into the lobby. At the east end there was a larger room. The plan shows the ages of the children taught in each room.

The area referred to as the lobby served a variety of purposes. It was a staff room, the School Secretary had her desk there, and the Headmaster also had his desk there, facing her on the other side of the room. There were storerooms for stationery and art materials, chairs for the staff and cupboards for books for staff use. This was not a very satisfactory situation as the head could never really have any privacy, nor could the staff or secretary. Nevertheless, we all seemed to manage reasonably well. In later years, by scrapping a storeroom and building out into the angle formed by the outer walls of the lobby and a classroom, the Head gained a room of his own, the small flat-roofed extension on the south front of the building.

At the east end of the building was a small garden laid out with a lawn and a pond. The bank towards the Infants' School playground had been terraced, much of the work done when the when the school educated boys up to the age of 14. The Headmaster had beehives in the garden and some boys used to help with them. On one occasion he had the whole school watching while he captured a swarm of bees and put it in an empty hive.

On the west side of the building were the toilets, necessitating a trip outside to visit them, and discouraging loitering there in the winter. The staff toilets were also outside. A path led into the playground. The younger boys played here and the older boys played out on the common between the playground wall and the Redhill Laundry which stood there then. The Head was very keen on cricket and every day in the lunch hour would go out and bowl for the boys.

When I began at St John's the classroom furnishings had not changed since my own schooldays. For a few years I had a high chair with a step, and a high desk with a lift-up lid and a cupboard under. There was not a lot of room and the lid slopped so one had to be tidy. I could stand on the step and look over the boy's heads. The boys sat at desks that had cast iron frames, a tip-up plank seat and a sloping lift-up top with a shelf underneath for books. There were two holes for inkwells and a groove for pens and pencils. There was a blackboard and easel and various bookcases and cupboards.

Teaching was very much chalk and talk but we also had filmstrips and slides and a 16mm projector. One was not allowed to use this equipment without the appropriate SCC course, which I had to do within my first few weeks.

A typical day would be as follows: - The boys arrived at 8.55 am and registration was at 9.00 am. If it was Monday dinner money was collected. At about 9.10-15 am the partitions between the three classrooms went back, the boys from the three other classes filed in and fitted in the spaces between desks etc. and so it became an assembly hall. Hymns were sung to piano accompaniment, prayers were said and the head would tell a suitable story or bible story. Following this the boys would return to their classes, the partitions would go back and morning teaching began. The first lesson was usually RE followed by maths. Morning break came next and then more lessons, possibly English.

There were no canteen facilities at the Boys' School (although the girls and infants had a place in the basement of their building) so at midday the boys would assemble in their playground and set off two by two under the supervision of two teachers along Pendleton Road, past St John's Church as far as the straight stretch before Sandpit Road was reached. The two teachers would cross the road and check it was clear and then, on a blast from a whistle, the boys would run across en masse. Then it was down to the Brighton Road. Here one teacher would step out into the road and stop the traffic, a daunting prospect although in later years we had a road patrolman to do it. The boys would run across and into St John's Parochial Hall for their lunch. This came in containers from the Colesmead Kitchen. The two duty teachers supervised lunch but the rest of the staff ate there as well. When all was finished the boys returned to school the same way.

Afternoon school included history, geography, art and craft and music - not all on the same day, of course. There was no curriculum as such; the Head compiled a syllabus and one largely taught from the text books in the class and anything else that interested one at the time. One was free to

The 1961 Cup-winning football team of 10 and 11 year-olds. In the back row from left to right are: - Mr Mitchell, Headmaster; Derek Stidder; Brian Potts; ? Cornish; Neil Frogg; unknown; Roderick Doller; Mr J.Beales. In the front are: - Martin Tompson; David Gellatly; Nigel Twivey, Captain; ? Chudley; and ? Tutt. The boy Cornish was the son of Den Cornish, referred to in Bertie House's 1930s reminiscences, and who played football for Redhill and Southall. The Boys were trained by Mr Beales and Mr Nevy. Derek Stidder has written books on watermills in the south of England.
Picture courtesy of Mr J.Beales

do anything relevant.

If it was a day for PE then this took place in the playground if fine. There was a variety of small apparatus for various activities. Once a week there was games. In the winter it was football, in the summer cricket or rounders. Our venue for games was either the upper lawn (the level area of common off Sandpit Road) or the pitch on the Ring. The lawn was reasonable for football, although rarely cut by the Council, but it was impossible to play cricket or rounders there as the ball was always lost. The common or the Ring was much better except the pitches there were full size and the boys looked lost on them. The other problem with the common was Mr Gould, the Common Keeper. In his peaked cap he looked rather like Hitler and acted like him; wherever we played we were we were always in the wrong and sent somewhere else. The boys used to change before leaving school and take their clothes with them, changing on the common and going home from there.

The District Sports were held in June. All junior schools in the area closed and went to Redhill Memorial Sports Ground, most to watch and some to compete, the teachers supervising sports and children. This continued for many years. The other District event was the Swimming Gala held at Redhill Swimming Baths in the London Road. This took place in the evening in the summer and the smell of chlorine and the noise echoing from the tiled walls was sure to give one a headache. St John's used to send a team to this and young teachers were expected to help out.

The other sporting event was the school's own sports day held at the end of the summer term. The school had a house system so competition took place on that basis. Sports Day was held on the upper lawn. For this the grass would be cut and a running track marked out. There was just room to fit in 100 yards and about four lanes in width. After lunch on the appointed day the whole school would leave carrying games equipment, tables, and chairs and benches for parents to sit upon. The Head would be carrying his 'public address system', a sheet of card rolled into a cone which he would shout through. An enjoyable afternoon would be had by all, followed by ice-cream all round at the Head's expense.

While on the subject of sports I must mention that the football team won the District Football Cup in 1961. The team was trained by Mr Brian Nevy and myself and was almost unbeaten through the 1960-61 season. Matches were played in school time (unlike today). We travelled to away matches by public transport (no school mini-buses then) and played on a variety of pitches. Home matches were played on the Ring. St John's and Furzefield had their own pitches. We played Horley Junior School on Horley Recreation Ground and Merstham Junior School on Merstham Recreation Ground but Holmesdale School we played on a pitch at the corner of Reigate Hill and Brokes Road, now long since built on.

At the end of my first (probationary) year Miss Buchan-Sydserff came to see me teaching and the outcome was that I passed and became fully qualified. It was a very easygoing system then, unlike today with frequent visits from inspectors. In my six years at the school I taught class 2a (7-8 years old), class 1b/2b (7-9 years old), then I had the same class through three years, 2a, 3a, 4a - not a good idea as one gets thoroughly tired of the same faces for three years. They get tired of the same teacher as everyone has a different style and different strengths and weaknesses. Finally I had 3a again.

There were 3 separate schools on the site, each with its own Head and staff. The Boys' School had very little association with the Girls' School but as some of our intake came from the Infants' School there was a little more liaison with the staff there. In 1956 the Infants' Head was Miss Kirkham but she was soon replaced by Mrs Tharp.

Staff of the Boys' School when I started in 1956 was Mr S.Mitchell, Head; Mr Ross, Deputy Head; Mr Browning; Mr Lofts; Mr O'Hagan; Mrs Richardson and myself. In due course Mr Ross retired and was replaced by Mr P D Pratt, who was eventually Head of Tatsfield and Reigate Priory Middle School. Mr Lofts died in 1957. Mr Brian Nevy eventually joined the staff as did Mr S Burchett. Later on Mr O'Hagan left and Mr Russ and Mr Llewelyn joined us. Another young teacher fresh from college was Miss Sylvia Hope-Scott. Mrs D James was the School Secretary.

Mr Ross had served in the Scots Guards during WW1 and when I knew him was at the end of his career. He had stayed in the School when the Church School moved out in 1954. He suffered from angina but this did not prevent him from smoking, a habit that caused a few minor diversions such as setting fire to the staff room waste paper basket and to the holly hedge at the front of the school. He retired in 1957 but sadly did not enjoy a long retirement as he died 18 months later.

Mr Nevy was a violinist and as we did not have a music teacher at that time would lead the hymns in assembly on the violin. Mr Burchell was a pianist and when he came both would play for assembly. Headteacher Mr Mitchell had spent most of his career in secondary schools. He was very helpful to me.

In 1956 the 11+ system was still in operation and although St John's C of E creamed off most of the best of the local boys we usually were able to get a few boys through to Grammar School each year. Those who passed went to Reigate, Dorking or Oxted. For the rest it was Secondary Modern education, and the choices were Earlswood, Frenches Road or the Reigate Priory. 11+ exams were taken within the school on a special day in the Spring Term (January or February). Only the classes actually taking the exam went to school, everyone else got the day off. There was also a grand moving round of teachers as one did not mark the papers in one's own school. When the new secondary school opened at Woodhatch in 1958 everyone was very keen to go there. Some parents moved their children to St John's as they thought it would give them a better chance.

Over the time I taught at St John's numbers slowly declined and by 1962 I thought I ought to move on as the school was threatened with closure and amalgamation with St John's Girls'. I obtained a post at St John's C of E at Reigate where I remained for the next 30 years, a symbol of continuity through three changes of Head and two changes of name until 1992. In the event the Boys' School remained until 1964 when Mr Mitchell retired.

Gordon Mackay

Gordon left the area in 1991 and eventually settled in Queensland, Australia with his family, where he owns an IT business. At the time of writing he was compiling a class poster with all the pictures of the pupils in his 4th year (1967/8 Mr Page), the idea being to distribute it free of charge to all of them.

Ex-Pupil Gordon Mackay, shown here when at Reigate Grammar School

He was born at Redhill General Hospital and lived at Heston Road Redhill until aged about 9. The house was a 'prefab' as they were called. These were buildings put up temporarily after WW2 to ease the housing shortage. They were made from asbestos sheet sandwiched with straw in the middle. All were identical in every way. Four children slept in one bedroom with their parents in the other. Only 2 bedrooms. Theirs was one of the last families to leave the prefabs in 1964 when they were dismantled and sold to Billy Butlins.

While at St John's he was a choir boy at St Johns Church. He used to get his bus fares paid to and from church for practices at the rate of 2 shillings and sixpence for weddings and 3 shillings for funerals. He never could work out why we got more for funerals.

Gordon's reminiscences

'The nature walks stick in my mind. We use to frequently go up onto the common to learn about the sticky buds on trees or be fascinated by the helicopter design of falling seeds from the trees. We had wonderful views from the top of the common. I don't think there is enough hands-on learning nowadays; all books and computers.

I remember getting a little bottle of milk every day and having the option of buying either 4 rich tea or 4 lincoln biscuits for 1d. Or if you were flush, a chocolate digestive individually wrapped in blue silver paper for milk or red for plain, I think they were a penny and a half each. I loved singing so morning assemblies were always something to look forward to, plus the annual Christmas Carol concert. The 3rd year really made a difference to me that has stayed with me all my life. Miss Tate was the most inspirational teacher I ever had. I had always been clever, top of the class in most things, great at all sports and a regular tough guy. I never had to have a fight in the school playground. Every one assumed I would knock their block off. I think it was because I was the baby of my family and had 2 older sisters and an older brother who taught me everything earlier in life than most. But being clever is one thing; knowing how to use it was what Miss Tate taught me, and not being a bighead but being confident - before her I didn't know there was a difference. About the only thing I have never been good at was art and she even made me feel good about myself with that. As an example, I was meant to be carving a face from a large block of chalk and on hitting it hard with a hammer and chisel it broke straight down the centre. She looked it and saw a thing of beauty. I couldn't understand then but as long as she thought it was good that was enough for me. She also knew how to handle me. She was very firm but fair. She was simply fantastic and I would love to tell her myself how I feel and what an inspiration she was to a little tough guy.

I did return to St Johns in my late teens to visit the school during a school day. The staff very kindly took me round. It was one of those nostalgic days. How small those toilets looked and so was everything else including the teachers.'

NOTE: - It was Gordon Mackay who, in July 2002, tracked down the British Pathé News archive of the art work done by St John's Boys on the walls of the air-raid shelter.

Children in the library in 1967. The three girls in the left-hand group are, from l-r, Ann Wood, Jacqui Stephens and Linda Tipping. Linda's mother was head dinner lady and also helped with playground duty. The boy at the back looking at the pictures is Tim Formoy. The girl centre of the right-hand group is Katherine Formoy Picture courtesy Linda Tipping

A production of Little Red Riding Hood in 1963. Brian Coomber is standing front centre of the boy's group. The girls front left represented flowers. Top left flower is Rose Day and Rowena next to her (I think). The middle row I am not sure of except the girl with the darker skin was Mandy who went to live in Ghana, and next to her a girl called Susan Edge who was a year younger. Bottom row is Jill Farrow, Sheila Harbour, Lorraine Greenfield, Leslie Coomber , Judith - possibly Dixon, Carol Dench, Sally Smith and myself, aged 6. At the back Elizabeth Wooten is Little Red Riding Hood and Anne Wood has the broom. The only other boy I remember was Philip Hood, probably because his parents had the sweet shop quite near to the school and I think they provided the lollies on sports day on the common. Picture and text courtesy Linda Tipping

Continuing into the 1970s

In 1972 Mrs Houseman left the Infants' School creating a vacancy for Deputy Head that was filled by Mrs Elphick. This was a time when Surrey was introducing the recommendations of the Plowden Report as St John's changed from a County Primary and Junior School to a First School, and as from 5th March 1973 the First School, with children aged from five to eight years, occupied the whole of the site. After the change to First School status the Headteacher, Mrs Tharp, lectured to visiting groups and travelled to other schools to lecture on 'The Breakthrough to Maths' and 'The Breakthrough to Literacy', new concepts of the time perhaps akin to the Literacy and Numeracy initiatives that were to come in the late 1990s

Managing Body meetings were still held alternately at Earlswood and St John's Schools. Mr Pringle, who had been the Chairman for many years retired on 20th June 1973. The Autumn term of that year began with a child with spina bifida, a child with cerebral palsy, a child with leukemia and a child with epilepsy in the First School. They presented special problems that needed special solutions, and perhaps their presence was a small experiment in a type of inclusive schooling that had not been seen before.

On 14th November 1973 there was a day's holiday for the wedding of Princess Anne. On 19th July Mrs Tharp retired after 16 years at the school - *'all happy'*, she wrote in the logs - delighted that her own deputy, Mrs Elphick, had been appointed in her place. Mrs Tharp was back in the November for a performance of *'Peter and the Enchanted Princess'* by the Globe Players. She died in 2001.

A new parent Manager, Mrs P.Horsfall, was appointed on the 4th December 1974. She has returned in recent years on a number of occasions in her role as a County Councillor. In 2000 her daughter, Tarn, was appointed a Governor.

In 1975 a new reference library was started with £200 worth of books from the County Library at Esher. During these few years a number of break-ins and acts of vandalism occurred but none caused any serious damage or loss. Most were at night but on 14th May 1975, the caretaker chased a man seen breaking into the Head's car during the day and with the help of the police he was caught. Only four days later a man was seen breaking into the school, during the day again. The police were again called but this time the intruder was not found. Letters delivered to the school were taken from the padlocked post box on two weekend occasions and deliveries were requested to be stopped on a Saturday as a consequence — but not before a fire was started in the box, with any mail present being destroyed. In any event Saturday deliveries did not cease and the rifling of the post box continued from time to time. Lead was stolen from School roofs on three

Staff of 1974
Back Row: - Mary Saddington, Val Johnson, Margaret Robinson, Cecelee Hawkins (secretary) Mary Freehold, Jane (surname unknown), Barbara Skevington, Barbara Llewellyn.
Front Row: - Micky Seymour, Pat Elphick, (Head 1974-87), Olive Tharp (Head 1958-74), Sue Keen, Dorothy Spalding.
Picture courtesy Olive Tharp

occasions in 1977 and break-ins continued. On 21st October 1977 the school had to be evacuated because of a bomb threat. The children were taken to the church until it was pronounced safe to return. June 2nd, the Queen's 25th Jubilee, was celebrated in School with various special activities, although cold weather for June relegated a planned picnic on the common to the school hall. Each child was presented with a Jubilee mug and Bible. Later in the month the two fourth year classes visited London and saw the Jubilee decorations.

In 1978 plans were seen at the Area Education Office in which St John's was classed as 'sub-standard' and scheduled for closure. Given that this was at a time when cuts in the County education budget were in force to the point where the caretaker had been on two courses regarding efficiency and savings of heating and lighting costs; that there were eight classes on site that would require a whole new school to house them, and that history has already shown us that St John's had weathered many crises before, the probability of closure was (despite our perfect hindsight) extremely unlikely. Besides, the school was rewired in this same year of 1978, a small give-away that closure was not really a serious threat.

If there *was* anything sub-standard about the school it was that it still had outside toilets in this day and age. In November 1978 a sub-committee of the Governing Body expressed concern about the matter in writing to the Chief Education Officer. Incidentally, this reference in the logbook contains the first mention of the 'Governing Body', a group of persons which hitherto had always been referred to as the 'Managers', although this remained an isolated reference until 1981 when the term 'Managers' seems to have finally been dropped.

Mrs Jagtiani, up to now a part-time teacher, started on 3rd January 1979 in the full-time post vacated by Mrs Parkinson leaving to have her first child. She immediately had two days off as the boiler broke down on 4th and 5th January and the school was closed. Repairs were less than fully effective and the school closed again on 23rd and 24th and gas heaters were placed in classrooms to supplement the struggling boiler, just as well as heating problems persisted into February. The problems concerned with keeping the school warm in winter has been a recurring theme in this history. The once recurring theme of problems though bad weather hardly receives a direct mention in modern logs, although a film crew who came in April to use the playground (reason unspecified) were unable to do for this reason.

After fourteen years as School Secretary Mrs Hawkins was replaced by Mrs Wetherall at the beginning of summer term of 1979. Miss Rawlins married and became Mrs Hildyard, and Miss Skevington visited a school at Turners Hill in connection with an application for Deputy Head there. The decade came to an uncertain end with the Deputy Head, Mrs Freehold, attending a talk at the Priory School by the Deputy Chief Education Officer about forthcoming cuts in teaching staff.

Chapter Eleven
The Final Decades of the 20th Century

Latter part of the Century

1980 was marked by school trips that almost all took place in continuous rain. This and falling numbers on role indicative of a falling birth rate and alterations to local catchment areas, plus the commencement of the sale of milk to children, characterised 1980.

1981 began with staff and the 150 children on roll again having to suffer boiler breakdown. An early log records, *'County Architects and a person from the Accommodation section at County Hall visited the school to draw up plans for ten new toilets to be sited INSIDE the school premises.'* Even without the word written in capitals and underlined this was clearly a major event in the history of the school, and surprisingly in an era which today might be regarded as relatively modern. That it actually *was* a relatively modern era is borne out by class 4S, in the same month of June, going to the Redhill Technical College to see the computers there. This is the first mention of these products of the electronic age that are so taken for granted today in office, school and home alike; the computer upon which this history has been compiled being just one example.

In the following July the Prince of Wales and Diana Spencer were married. A fun day was held at school in celebration but a planned picnic had to be held inside because of rain. Heavy rain might have been more welcome a few nights previously when a school shed went up in flames with the loss of £500 of school furniture.

In September, *'the Chairman of Managers Governors met to approve the plans for the ten new toilets to be built inside the school.'* Mrs Hense and Mrs Coulson were Chair and Deputy Chair of Governors at the time, and building work began in January of 1981, with the official hand-over on April 5th. The Governing Body at this time was concerned with three schools: - St John's First, Earlswood First and Brambletye Middle.

The relationship between Church and School, despite changes occurring over the years, has always been a continuous one and the Vicar of these times, the Rev. Goss, was a regular visitor.

By the 1982 autumn term the number on roll had fallen to 136 (compare this to 730 at the school in 1902) a number that rose to 156 in 1983 and 188 in 1984. During this latter year Mrs Freehold left to take up a headship elsewhere and Mrs Cruickshank came on supply to take her class. Mrs Burgess was appointed Deputy

The 1983 opening of the new adventure area

The School on the Common

Head in place of Mrs Freehold.

Projects such as the foam insulation of cavity walls, the installation of a sink unit in the staff room and an adventure playground got off the ground. The latter, constructed by parents, was opened on September 17th. A boy had a tooth knocked out while playing on it in November and was treated in hospital, although this is not to say it was a particular hazard as within four days of the incident another boy was taken to hospital to have stitches put in a cut sustained by banging into a wall, and a girl slipped and fell into a playground wall and broke her arm. In January 1984 a boy slipped on ice and broke his wrist.

1984 boys dressed in the style of 1884

In February 1984 the Assistant Area Education Officer came to discuss plans for a car park on common land, a sign of the times and presumably the same car park that in 1999 had swingeing restrictions imposed upon it by the local authorities. 1984 was the year of the teachers' strike - two classes were set home as a result.

On May 24th *'100 years of the school'* was celebrated, based on the date over the door of the lower building. It was a whole day of celebration during which included a thanksgiving service in church. Children and teachers dressed up as Victorians and entertained 2-300 guests with a picnic, games and various other activities. There was also a museum of artefacts and a slide show of times gone by. Good weather enabled all activities to be fulfilled. School started an hour late the following day to allow time for clearing up.

On July 16th 1984 a log states simply *'The micro-computer arrived in school.'* Can we presume this to be the first of its kind? Certainly there is no previous mention of computers other than visits to view those at the Technical College, so maybe this was the first step taken by St John's into the electronic age, something we now feel is well and truly with us but is in many ways perhaps only still beginning. Staff attended a BBC Acorn computer course in September.

St Matthew's First School closed in July '84 and its deputy head was seconded to St John's. Reference to 'the car parking problem' heralded an ongoing saga perhaps not realised at the time.

Staff at St John's School 1989, the year the National Curriculum was implemented.

Peter Wood,	Head
Maggi Livingstone	Deputy Head
Ann Cruickshank	Language Co-ordinator
Moira Brown	CDT and Art Co-ordinator
Joan Jagtiani	RE +
Cathy Dyson	SEN Co-ordinator
Elizabeth Horner	Music Co-ordinator
Rosemary Harvey	Maths Co-ordinator + other school links
Molly Weatherall	Senior School Assistant
Carol Carpenter	School Assistant
Ray Nightingale	Caretaker
7 classes	3 comprising reception & year 1, 2 year 2's and 2 year 3's

School helper Mrs Pat Hamilton retired at the end of spring term after 23 years at the school, her place being taken by Mrs Carol Carpenter. Summer term began with 210 children, the highest number for five years, an extra class (white) made up of reception children being formed with Mrs Cruickshank as its teacher.

Brighton Dolphinarium, Outwood Mill, Reigate Priory Museum, Charlwood Zoo, Bluebell Railway; these were some of a number of local attractions where outings continued to go to. The London attractions were still also included. Between January and March 1987 the School was broken into 5 times. A large Elm tree fell across the path to the lower building in May '87, perhaps an omen of the storm of October that year, the worst for three hundred years, when more trees and the school's TV aerial came down. Tiles were also blown from the roof and the school was closed until October 20th.

On December 18th 1987 the Headteacher, Mrs Elphick retired after thirteen and a half happy years at the school. Her last words in the logbook were, *'Long may St John's flourish.'*

In February 1998 the St John's members of the three-school Governing Body were outvoted in their desire to create a separate body of governors for their school. Mr Easton, the caretaker, retired in April, and was replaced by Ray Nightingale in September. At the same time new Headteacher Peter Wood from inner London took up his post along with new teacher Catherine Dyson. Mrs Robinson, who had been at St John's 17 years, left at the end of the year.

A great deal of work was necessary to prepare for the implementation of the National Curriculum and by the end of 1989 concern was being expressed over the planning and record procedures - time taken to account instead of teach - and the tiredness and low morale of the staff. The recently formed Friends of St John's held their first social event, a barn dance, in October while in November influenza almost closed the school, with staff and children alike affected and pupil attendance falling from over 200 to well below 100. The close of 1989 also saw the close of the log book in which events since 1954 had been recorded. The final words written were, *' The end of a tiring and stressful term.'*

The morning of January 25th 1990 saw a storm almost as intense as the one of October 1987. Children had to be escorted between the buildings in small groups, such was the strength of the wind. Roof damage occurred in several places. Repairs were still not complete a week later when a part of green class ceiling collapsed due to damage to the lead and tiles on the roof above it that had not been spotted.

The installation of toilets in the lower building was completed and at the end of the summer term both the Head, Peter Wood, and teacher Rosemary Harvey, left, the latter to become deputy Head at Furzefield First School, Merstham. Maggi Livingstone filled the Head's post in an acting capacity until the new appointment, Mrs Gent, came to take over at the beginning of the new term in January.

The start of Mrs Gent's time at the school was dogged by problems. First boiler malfunctions took a few days to put right and then some of the school's computers were found on the common during the middle weekend of January. Inside the school it was discovered that a fire had been started in the centre of the upper building. Fire and smoke damage was considerable and the school had to be closed for a week while cleaning, repairs and furniture and carpet replacements were made. It was not until March that the clean-up process ended, and redecoration was still required. It was a testing time for all staff, of which Mrs Gent was not the only new member, Mrs Cotton having started as the new Administration Officer on January 14th.

Things did get better - but slowly and certainly not right away. Two teenagers were caught stealing from the lower building in February, money was short for redecorating, and reorganisation regarding new arrangements for age of transfer was in hand. One thing that always seemed to go well was the school sports, which were usually blessed with fine weather. For many years - since the war, in fact - they had been held on the Lawns on Redhill Common but now returned to the Ring for the first time since then.

During the summer holidays all the rooms were carpeted and much of the redecoration done. Another change that had occurred, albeit in the broader period since the late 1980s, was the

Governing Body separating from Earlswood and Brambletye Schools and becoming exclusive to St John's. Mr Waller was Chairman at this time but was replaced by John Coulson in October 1992, with Jane Forbat as Deputy Chair. Caretaker Ray Nightingale resigned at the beginning of 1992 and was replaced by John Clarke.

St John's First Baptist Primary School, Likoni, Kenya

In 1993 St John's Church member Angela Prentice and her husband Mike went on holiday to Kenya and were very moved by the number of child beggars they saw there. Many of these children had been orphaned in a ferry disaster a year earlier when 300 perished, leaving many families without a breadwinner. Likoni is a port area and there is a very high death rate from Aids, leaving many of these children destitute.

When Angela and Mike returned home they could not forget these children and their desperate plight. Through contacts they had made at their holiday hotel they were put in touch with Pastor Wellington, who was involved with helping the local children. His dream was to educate the children to help them escape from their poverty. Angela and Mike sent him money and with this he set up a small school with just one teacher and 35 pupils. Six months later Pastor Wellington wrote to Angela and Mike asking for more money to expand the school. They decided to make another visit to Shonda to see how the money they planned to raise could be best spent. This time, when they arrived in the village, they were greeted by a song of welcome from the children in the small school. The village officials wanted to name the school Angela's School, but eventually it was named St John's First Baptist Primary School. Whilst there, Angela and Mike took many photographs, which they planned to show to the parishioners of St John's Church to start fund raising. In 1997 The Shonda Project became a registered charity.

In her role of pastoral visitor, Angela frequently visits Redhill St John's School, and by talking to the staff and children and showing them her photographs a link was forged between the two schools which continues to flourish today. Parents are encouraged to sponsor children. Outgrown school uniform is collected and other events, such as cake and book sales, are organised to raise much-needed funds. Collections are made of essential stationery items, which Angela and Mike take with them on their annual visit, not to mention the footballs that are joyously received each time they go! Redhill St John's teacher, Ann Cruickshank, visited the Shonda school a few years ago to advise and assist the teaching staff there. The older children of both schools keep in touch by letters.

In past years the school has started a feeding project to make sure that the children have at least one nutritious meal a day. A well has been sunk which ensures clean drinking water for the local village and the school.

At the beginning of the 21st century the fund raising becomes even more vital as the African school expands and its fame spreads. Plans are in hand to set up a training college for the pupils as they finish their education. A full-page spread in the Reigate and Redhill Life newspaper resulted in a collection of old sewing machines from local people anxious to help. Further funding and assistance is always welcome.

Changes Continue

Administrator Molly Weatherall retired at the end of 1993, having started at St John's in the late 1960s, and the office was reorganised with Mrs Cotton and Carol Carpenter covering her duties as from the beginning of 1994. Staff at this time were: Headteacher, Mrs Gent; Deputy, Maggi Livingstone; Teachers, Alison Turnbull, Joan Jagtiani, Cathy Dyson, Sue Hayward, Elizabeth Horner, Ann Cruikshank, and Ann Tompkin. Admin staff were Shirley Cotton, Carol Carpenter and the caretaker was John Clarke.

In April of 1994 the conversion of the old outside toilet block (which might have been built in 1910 but could have been earlier) into a music and drama room was begun by parents.

In June 1994 contractors had begun work in preparation for the 'Age of Transfer', the re-organisation of the School from a First to a Primary School. Children still attended in reception class as 'rising fives' but the age range was now generally 5-11. Due to numbers coming in at year 1 two classes started, meaning that this 'bulge' of two classes would continue through the school until they left at the end of their year 6 in 2000.

In December 1995 there was the official opening of the new Music and Drama room with visit of personality Dave Benson Phillips, who was appearing in Snow White pantomime at the Harlequin Theatre, Redhill.

In May 1996 the Ofsted inspectors descended upon the School. In spite of the School being a well-run and successful establishment their inspection left its mark, as any close scrutiny might upon those who endured it, and it is to be wondered how inspection in days of old affected the School. Ofsted inspections are an aspect of modern education, however, and the inspectors' report was received by the Governing Body and staff in a positive manner, accepting praise where due and ready to act to correct criticism. Although

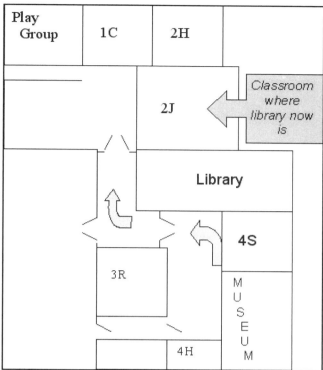

Changes made to upper building
This diagram is based on the plan of the upper building as shown in the 1984 centenary celebration programme.

the Headteacher recorded a number of problems mainly associated with the administration of the building and paperwork for this year, she also recorded that it had been a successful year with regard to educational achievements.

The death of a pupil is always an extreme blow to any school. At St John's in November 1996 a boy who had suffered from leukaemia for a number of years was given a helicopter flight locally, passing over the school with all the children outside in the playground waving to him. Sadly he died in January 1997. A plaque was put on a new bench by the pond in his memory.

February 1997 was when sex education began for year 6. Two months later Headteacher Cynthia Gent was replaced by Tony Richardson, already a Head at a Croydon school who wanted to transfer to the Redhill area. In July the first stirrings of the parking problems began.

Also beginning was a new scheme whereby each class adopted a governor. That governor then began a special relationship with that class, remaining with it as it progressed through the school. Examples of activities include reading stories on school visits, sending postcards and emails to the class when on holiday, donating useful and/or interesting items encountered to the class. New developments this year and in 1998 were the instigation of Literacy and Numeracy hours in the school, a Government initiative.

In January 1996 there had been the first visit by an official regarding the possibility of converting the staff room into a classroom and building new offices onto the building. This was due to the identification of the need to expand a local school to accommodate an increase in numbers of children, and St John's had been chosen as that school. The possible growth of the school was an ongoing subject, with both buildings involved, until a change of mind due to objections regarding the highways occurred in 1998.

In past years classroom assistants had been engaged to supplement and complement the work done in classes. These additional, part-time members of staff were, and still are, paid from the annual school budget, and if cuts become necessary to that budget then their hours might well be

Governor Jeremy Wilson collects the cup for the best float in the 1994 Reigate Carnival from the Mayor. The float is shown in the lower picture with Teacher Mrs Cruickshank and children aboard

Mrs Jagtiani (left) on the occasion of her retirement. Headteacher Mrs Gent is in conversation with Deputy Ms Livingstone (seated).

where some of those cuts fall. This was precisely the situation in 1999 when an unexpected shortfall in the money provided to school by central government led to cuts having to be made in this area. In July of this year Maggi Livingstone left and due to the cutbacks, the post of Deputy Head was left vacant. This was the beginning of a difficult period, especially for the Head, Tony Richardson, who had recently resigned his post due to ill health but not yet left. Not only did that loss of a deputy throw extra work upon the him but another Ofsted inspection in November, which he agreed to stay to see through, added to his load. That inspection also revealed some weaknesses within the system that caused further problems, not least for the new incoming Headteacher who, also without a deputy, would have to manage. These difficulties were not the best note on which to end the millennium (the popular view had it that the millennium ended on December 31st 1999) but Tony Richardson's last log entry remained hopeful for the future. *'I hope St John's continues to prosper and improve',* he wrote. *'The children, parents and governors have helped to create an excellent environment. I am grateful for their support.'* And another head departed, this time after two years and two terms at the school, although with a total of sixteen years of headship behind him altogether.

Chapter Twelve
A New Millennium

Up-to-date

Many things are now very different from days gone by. The cabling of the computer system for example, 'walking buses' in this age of such busy roads, the Curriculum Committee discussing the Ofsted (Office of Standards in Education) Action Plan, and dinner supervisors judging the 'futuristic egg' competition. But many activities are the same or similar, such as football matches against other schools, medical inspections, the Vicar taking assembly, class outings, homework, exams - the list goes on.

One unusual event of 2000 was the enclosing, by the Council, of much of the land on the south side of the School used as a car park. This area had been created on common land over a number of years as the relatively isolated aspect of the school in the age of the car also created a demand for space for the dropping off and collection of children, as well as a parking place for staff. The replacement of the nearby laundry by houses in the latter part of the previous century created an additional and perhaps not uncritical body of neighbours where there were none before. The lay of the land between them - metaphorically as well as practically - created a situation where something had to be done. Unfortunately for St John's a restriction upon its use was the result.

A special event was the funding and opening of the Millennium Library. It was special because of the refurbished and renewed facility provided through the magnificent efforts and fund raising of the Friends of St John's.

In March Headteacher Miss Cassidy suggested that the School's history be written. Work began and the April opening of the new library was combined with a potted history of the school, a play by the children and a showing of slides from Mr Bertie House's collection from the

Here are the first words written in the current logbook by the new Headteacher, Miss Marian Cassidy.
School life picked up for another term where it had left off the previous one, just as it had done for the past one hundred and fifty-five year.

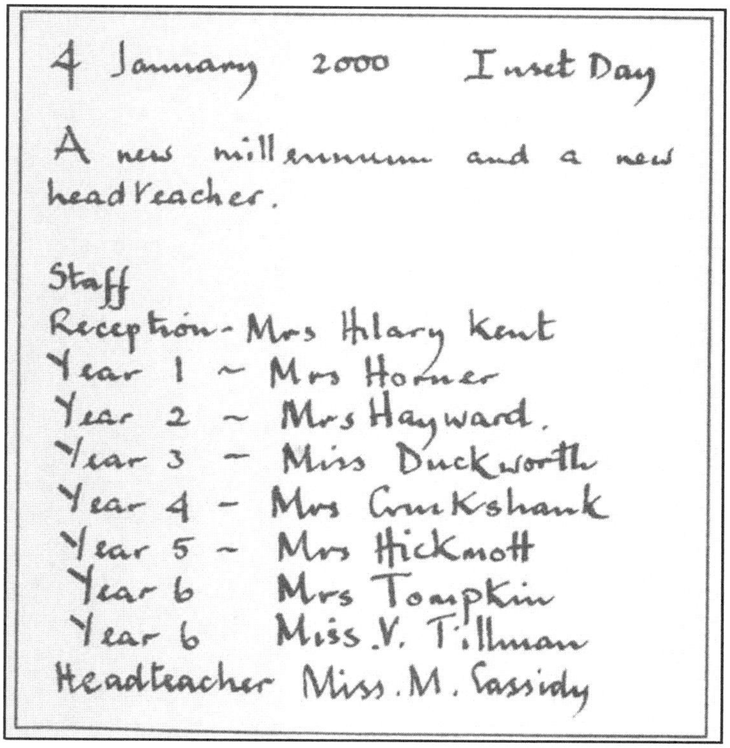

4 January 2000   Inset Day

A new millennium and a new headteacher.

Staff
Reception - Mrs Hilary Kent
Year 1 ~ Mrs Horner
Year 2 ~ Mrs Hayward.
Year 3 - Miss Duckworth
Year 4 - Mrs Cruikshank
Year 5 ~ Mrs Hickmott
Year 6   Mrs Tompkin
Year 6   Miss. V. Tillman
Headteacher Miss. M. Cassidy

School's past. Later in the year, on the 10th of July, a history evening was held. One hundred and fifty visitors, many of them past pupils and staff members on a nostalgic return, came to look around the buildings, listen to a talk about the history of St John's and see an extended version of Bertie House's slide show.

Later that year John Coulson retired as Chair of the Governing Body. He had been Chair for eight years and a Governor before that. John Clarke retired as caretaker in October. He had been a Governor for a part of his time at the School and had been very active with the football team. Like many others at St John's he had become a part of the place and would inevitably be missed.

Unfortunately John also missed out on something that might have added a little extra to his going. He was apt to write the odd poem and as a part of the research into the School's past for this history it had been discovered that Fleur Adcock OBE, a prominent poet of our time, had been a pupil at St John's during the war. As a consequence she was, through the BBC, invited to the history evening but did not get the message in time. She was upset about this as she had fond

memories of her old school and wanted to make a return visit. She had returned in the 1970s when school was closed, had peered through the railings and as a result had written and published a poem about the School. Attempts were made for her visit to coincide with John's retirement - thoughts of a special presentation by her to him - but her commitments were such that she was unable to make that date.

Fleur Adcock aged nine

Fleur eventually came to St John's on November 16th. She was able to look around the school, meet Mrs Barratt, who had been one of her teachers in the 1940s and who came in for the afternoon, talk to parents and staff and take a special assembly. It was a very memorable day for all concerned.

At the end of the summer term the last of the two-year intake left to go to secondary schools. For the first time for many years the summer term began with only seven classes, and a classroom fell vacant. Of the two teachers only one was now required and the adjustment was duly made. In October one of the Senior Management Team teachers resigned, something which, coupled with Government educational finance initiatives, paved the way for the re-appointment of a Deputy Headteacher. The post was advertised, interviews took place in December, and Sue Brabbins was appointed.

In the last week of November 2000 it was

Fleur Adcock (below) admiring some of the year 6 children's work with MrsTompkin in November 2000. Fleur's poem about the school appears in appendix 2.

discovered that the boiler chimney was blocked. The current gas-fired boiler had been installed in 1983 and it is possible that proper checks had not been carried out on the installation, including the chimney, for some, if all, of this time. A sweep was unable to get a brush to the top and scaffolding had to be erected so it could be swept from the top. A sackful of bird's-nests was retrieved and a cowl subsequently fitted to deny the home-building by our feathered friends being repeated.

A New Office

As the school passed into the year 2001 there were several important projects on the horizon, one of which was the provision of a new office. For many years the admin staff had worked in cramped conditions in the upper rooms at the west end of the upper building. Because they were away from the main entrance they could not monitor comings and goings and visitors to the school had to climb the stairs to see them. In spite of keypads having been fitted to the entrances in the late 1990s security would clearly benefit from the office being relocated to the vacant classroom adjacent to the main entrance. In addition to the security aspect there was the opportunity to enhance the facilities that a new, much larger office would provide. All that was needed was the money to carry out the work. Half came from the Government, the rest from the school budget.

The new office was ready for the 2004 Autumn term. It had a hatch with sliding glass doors opening onto the entrance corridor, improved facilities for administration staff and separate storage and sick bay areas.

The Queen's Jubilee

In 2002 the School celebrated the Queen's Jubilee. A whole day's events included sports on the common, a children's tea party in the playground and a fish and chip supper followed by a barn dance.

The School Clock

St John's School Clock in its modern setting

The St John's School clock was made in 1860 by Thwaites and Read, who also made the Westminster clock commonly known as Big Ben. The St John's clock was originally installed high in the tower of the first building on the school site and when that was demolished it was transferred to the present tower.

Over its many earlier years the clock gave good service but for several decades prior to 1973 was out of service until two local horologists, Peter Hawkins and Peter Johnson, undertook its restoration. The clock movement was full of pigeon droppings, all of which had to be removed before three months cleaning and restoration could be carried out. On a lovely day in May 1973 Headteacher Mrs Tharp invited the two clock restorers to a special gathering when the children were called to morning assembly by the ringing of the bell. A special 'School Clock Song' was sung. Afterwards everyone watched as the school caretaker Brian Hunt set the pendulum in motion and set the hands to time.

The clock is driven by two cast iron weights weighing 48lbs and 65lbs respectively, one for the going train the other for striking. The dials are each four feet across and the hours are struck on an eighteen-inch diameter bell housed above the clock movement. Winding of the two clock trains involves the climbing of a set of stone steps in the base of the clock tower and then four vertical ladders fixed to the inner sides of its walls. Following this climb of fifty-seven steps and rungs there is a struggle through a 16 x 22-inch opening up onto the winding platform.

Since 1976 this job was done on a voluntary basis by Bertie House, ex-pupil and local resident with an interest in clocks. He also carried out some of the work necessary when things went wrong with the mechanism. But in 1996 the Governing Body decided that Mr House could no longer be expected to carry out this task for safety reasons. The clock was accordingly stopped, its hands pointing to noon.

If the clock was not to be wound by hand then some other way of controlling it would have to be found. Governor Jeremy Wilson and the Friends of St John's began raising money for the purpose and looking into the merits of various means of alternative control. Eventually the firm of Thwaites & Reed, the original makers of the clock, were commissioned to provide a new clock system with replacement electric drives and a means of keeping the clock at the correct time.

The process took more than eight years, terminating - again on a lovely day - in September 2004, when Bertie House was invited to restart the clock. With Headteacher Miss Cassidy, children, Bertie and guests in the playground, the clock was restarted exactly at noon and the children counted out the twelve strikes of the its bell.

Today the clock continues to show the correct time, not just to the school but to the local community, any small variations in accuracy being corrected at noon each day by a radio signal from Frankfurt in Germany.

The Extension

There was another building project planned, that of the extension of the boys' toilets. That they were inside the building when once they had been outside was a great improvement but the area was also used as a cloakroom and this area needed enlarging. This was another major building project that required not only the money but additional expertise. The money came partly from the Government and partly from the school budget. Expertise came in the form of an architect, who liaised with the school, provided drawings, appointed an approved contractor to carry out the work and acted as Clerk of the Works. It was not a straightforward task; many decisions had to be made as to the layout and design of internal and external features within budgetary constraints. Finally the plans laid over two years came to fruition and the new extension at the front of the upper building was ready in October 2004.

Air Raid Shelters

The painting of the walls of the Boy's School air raid shelter is touched upon on page 88. The story of the 1941 manager's visit to the see the paintings and the subsequent filming of them came to light when the school logbooks were read in 2001 during the research for this book. When the shelter was closed following the end of the war is not recorded but was presumably shortly after. Whether it had been opened again in the meantime is not recorded either but certainly knowledge of the paintings' existence had been lost, so once known again the re-opening of the shelters was inevitable.

The shelters were opened in the Spring of 2003. Martyn Rout and this author went down expecting to find damp and muddy conditions and were amazed to find instead that the shelter was dry and fairly clear of debris. Moreover, the sixty-two year old paintings were remarkably well preserved, with their bright colours showing in our torchlight. Another surprise was the extent of the shelter's corridors and the amount of painting that had been done, with only a small area remaining unpainted. Most of the benches that had once lined the walls were gone but one or two remained as a reminder of those wartime days long ago when the shelters had to be occupied. First thoughts were that the paintings had been done to while away the time between air raid alerts but it was soon

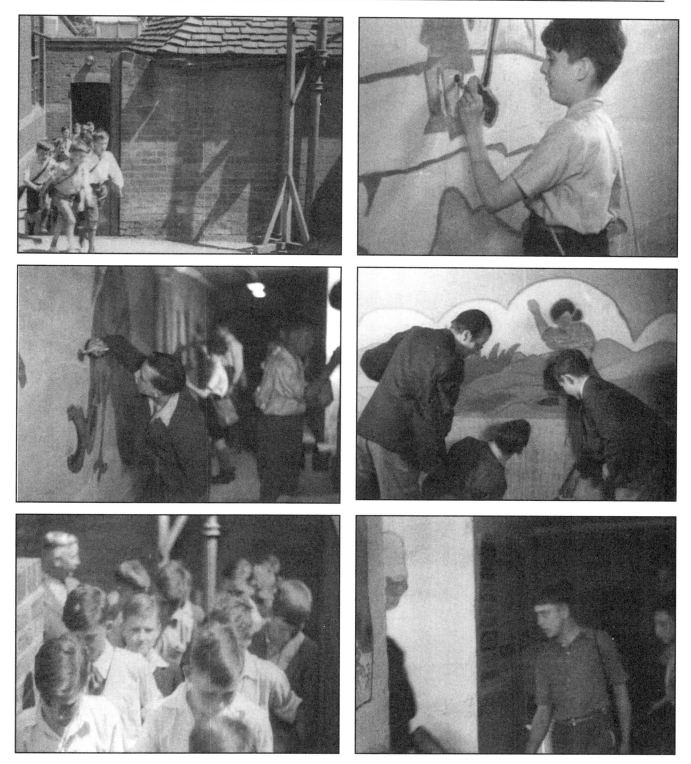

Stills from the footage filmed by Pathé News of St John's boys air raid shelter 1941. The paintings became national news at cinemas across the country.

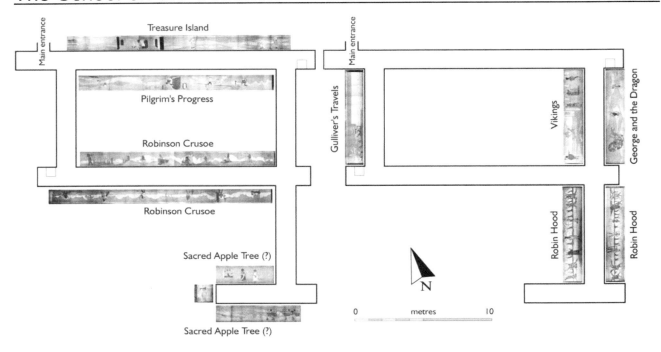

Treasure Island

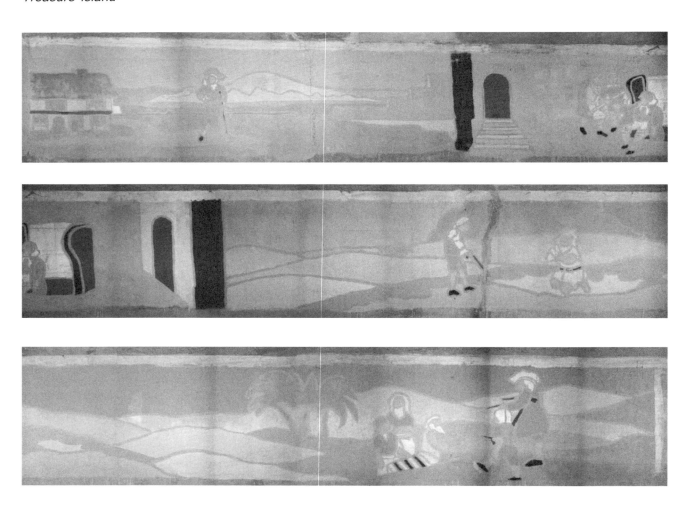

Pilgrims Progress

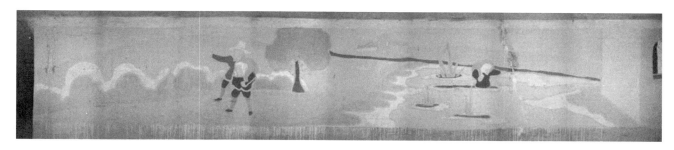

Robinson Crusoe

George and the Dragon

Our motif- The Dragon

The Vikings

Robin Hood

Sacred Apple Tree

The School on the Common

End Wall

Gulliver's Travels

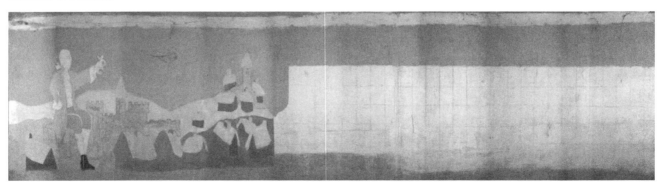

July 2005 St John's School Summer Fun Day, special guest Bill Pertwee

July 2005 current pupils re-enacting the air raid shelter drill

realised that there would simply have not been the room for the boys to fill the shelters and paint as well, so the paintings must have been carried out as part of the art classes of the day when the shelter was otherwise unoccupied.

The shelters were cleaned out, enquiries made as to their ownership and consideration given as to what was to happen next. The overhead lighting - long since disconnected from the mains and some of it detached from the ceiling – was kept where it was safe to do so. Ownership was claimed by Reigate Council with stewardship granted to the school.

In Spring 2005 the BBC came to film the shelter; researchers interviewing children, staff and this author, the resulting film being shown on BBC regional news. The shelter also featured on local radio when the St John's caretaker, and later in the year a School Governor, were interviewed.

On Saturday 2nd July 2005 the shelter was opened during the annual school fete, which had a WW2 theme to celebrate the 60th anniversary of VE Day. The opening ceremony was conducted by the Mayor of Reigate, Councillor Dixon. The occasion was enhanced by the presence of Dad's Army veteran Bill Pertwee, replete with genuine warden's tin helmet.

On the following day, Sunday 3rd, the school hosted the BBC who came to interview invited past pupils to record their wartime experiences for the BBC People's War website (bbc.co.uk/ww2)

The shelters used by the Girls' and Infants' School were opened but were found to have nothing of immediate interest and were re-closed. There are plans to revisit these shelters at a later date to re-examine them. The Boys' School shelter remains a fascinating remnant of those far off war days and a valuable asset for the present-day school. A lottery grant has been obtained to enable the shelter to be used as an educational resource and for it to be opened to the public on occasion. The money will also enable pupils to create a heritage-based resource in the form of an audio-visual record, taking advantage of the fact that the 1940s are still in living memory and using past pupils' wartime reminiscences. The condition of the shelter and the paintings is such that no restoration is necessary.

July 2005 re-enactment of gas mask drill

In Retrospect

1995 got a very short mention on early pages but in fact something was added to the school area that had a very noticeable presence, and that was the 20mph speed limit that was introduced to the normally 30mph part of Pendleton Road passing St John's. It was the first variable speed limit in Surrey and has been enforced at times when children and parents have to cross the Road and was a pilot study that, if successful, was to be used at other schools. Clearly everyone realises that caution needs to be taken at school sites and the scheme was universally praised.

To Top Everything Off

At an age of almost 100 years the roof of the upper building is at the end of its life. The amount of work necessary, with its accompanying potential for disruption to school life and the corresponding cost, presents the next challenge for St John's. The school has faced many challenges throughout its long history and will no doubt rise to this latest one.

Staff members as at January 2006:-

Headteacher	Miss M.Cassidy
Deputy Head	Miss G Steinthal
Reception Teacher	Miss L Forbes
Year 1 teacher	Mrs C Jackson
Year 2	Mrs F Hewett
Year 3	Miss G Steinthal
Year 4	Miss L Gopar
Year 5	Miss E Allen
Year 6	Mr A McGreevy
Senco	Mrs J Langford
Administration	Mrs D Bradford
Administration	Mrs M Smith
Caretaker	Mr M Rout

Although research has not been able to unearth every aspect of St John's School's considerable history, enough has come to light to show that it has enjoyed in excess of a century and a half of fruitful existence in one form or another.

However the school progresses may its future be as rich and memorable as its past ....

Heads of St John's (those known)

Boys' School

? ? Mr Dinner ?
– 1870 Mr Hale
1870 – 1874 Mr J.G.Scott
1874 – 1876 Mr A.Janney
1876 – 1919 Mr Jinks
1919 – 1919 (Temp) J.Lancaster
1919 – 1924 Mr O.Gregson
1924 – 1932 Mr H.C.Cole
1932 – 1953 Mr R.G.Bennett
1953 – 1954 Mr Boddington
1954 – 1964 Mr S.Mitchell

Girls' School

– 1872 Miss Vic
1872 – 1876 Miss Tilley (Janney)
1876 – 1901 Mrs Jinks
1902 – 1905 Miss A.M.Greening
1905 – 1915 C.M.Lansdell
1915 – 1919 A.C.Harvey
1919 – 1938 Miss Towell
1938 – 1953 Miss A.White
1953 – 1959 Miss Dudman
1959 – 1960 (acting) Mrs Mansell
1960 – 1964 Mrs MacNeil

Infants' School

1872 – 1873 Miss Tracy
1873 – 1874 (Temp) Miss Frew
1874 – 1875 Miss Denner
1876 – 1878 Miss Scott
1878 – 1901 Miss Spurway
1901 – 1903 Miss G.Franklin
1903 – 1933 Miss E.M.Whyman
1933 – 1950 Miss E.M.Faulkner
1950 – 1958 Miss J.Kirkham
1958 – 1972 Mrs O.Tharp

1964 - Boys' and Girls' depts. merge

1964 – 1965 Mrs MacNeil
1965 – 1966 (acting) Mrs Mansell
1966 – 1972 Mr Bowden

1972 - Infants' dept. merges with Boys' and Girls' depts.

1972 – 1974 Mrs O.Tharp
1974 – 1987 Mrs Elphick
1987 – 1988 (acting) Mrs M. Livingstone
1988 – 1990 Mr Peter Wood
1990 – 1991 (acting) Mrs M. Livingstone
1991 – 1997 Mrs Gent
1997 – 1999 Mr A.Richardson
2000 –   Miss M.Cassidy

St John's School

When I went back the school was rather small
but not unexpectedly or rather oddly so.
I peered in at the windows of the hall
Where we sang O God Our Help thirty years ago
for D-Day, the Normandy landings. It was all
As I'd pictured it. Outside they'd cut the row

of dusty laurels, laid a lawn instead,
And the prefab classroom at the end was new;
but there were the lavatories, there was the shed
where we sat on rainy days with nothing to do,
giggling; and the beech-trees overhead
whose fallen husks we used to rifle through

for triangular nuts. Yes, all as it should be -
no false images to negotiate,
no shocks. I wandered off contentedly
across the playground. Out through the north gate,
down the still knee-straining slope, to see
what sprang up suddenly across the street:

the church, that had hardly existed in my past,
that had lurked behind a tree or two, unknown -
and uncensorious of me as I chased
squirrels over the graves - the church had grown:
high on its huge mound it soared, vast:
and God glared out from behind a tombstone.

Fleur Adcock

This poem is reproduced with kind permission of Fleur
Adcock

MATTERS ARISING

A few miscellaneous items from the History of St John's

What's in a Name?

Sometimes people's names fit very well with what they do on occasion. Here is a reminder of those three examples of Boys' Schoolteachers.

Mr Hurt, who was dismissed for caning boys
Mr Bath, who took the boys swimming
Mr Weeds, who took the boys gardening

Words

It is always interesting to see how the language has changed over the years. In the period during which St John's Schools Logs have been written one would not expect to find much difference in word usage from today, but a few instances cropped up and are noted here.

Vacation When talking about the regular school breaks at Easter, Summer and Christmas 'vacation', a word we tend today to sometimes think of as an Americanism, is often used, whereas impromptu days off are invariably referred to as 'holidays'.
Overlooked Girls' School Log entry - *'June 8th 1893 Needle work examinations overlooked by Mistress'.* Presumably she supervised them and did not forget them or not notice they were going on.
Old-style Double s   Mistrefs (Mistress). We are accustomed to seeing the letter s written like a flowery f (f) in old writing. In the Committee logs of the 1870s the s is written normally except when ss appears. Then the first s is written f giving the appearance fs, for example as in Mistress above.

Gender

Words indicating the difference in gender are tending to be used less and less, so when examples such as Monitor and Monitress occur they stand out.

Misreading of hand-written entries

The logs are almost entirely written quite legibly but because of various styles one or two first-time misreadings occurred. Here are two examples that enforced a double take: -
Miss Kaffka was absent today as she is suffering from a child (chill)
Mrs Silly has come on supply (Selby)

MATTERS ARISING
Cont.

Misspellings

Spelling mistakes were so few that this was the only one noticed.

'One girl was sent home with a suspicious pealing of hands' - perhaps caused by too much bell ringing? (Although a spelling mistake is treated here with humour, peeling of skin of various parts of the body was a sign of scarlet fever. If the child in question knew this then it was no doubt a very worrying thing for them)

Chilldren - an ironic misspelling by the author when recording the poor health of the 1920s.

_____